Heroes

Robert Cormier

**Oxford
Literature
Companions**

Notes and activities: Su Fielder

OXFORD

UNIVERSITY PRESS

Contents

Introduction

What are Oxford Literature Companions?

Oxford Literature Companions is a series designed to provide you with comprehensive support for popular set texts. You can use the Companion alongside your novel, using relevant sections during your studies or using the book as a whole for revision.

Each Companion includes detailed guidance and practical activities on:

- **Plot and Structure**
- **Context**
- **Characters**
- **Language**
- **Themes**
- **Skills and Practice**

How does this book help with exam preparation?

As well as providing guidance on key areas of the novel, throughout this book you will also find 'UpGrade' features. These are tips to help with your exam preparation and performance.

In addition, in the extensive **Skills and Practice** chapter, the **Exam skills** section provides detailed guidance on areas such as how to prepare for the exam, understanding the question, planning your response and hints for what to do (or not do) in the exam.

In the **Skills and Practice** chapter there is also a bank of **Sample questions** and **Sample answers**. The **Sample answers** are marked and include annotations and a summative comment.

How does this book help with terminology?

Throughout the book, key terms are **highlighted** in the text and explained on the same page. There is also a detailed **Glossary** at the end of the book that explains, in the context of the novel, all the relevant literary terms highlighted in this book.

How does this book work?

Each book in the Oxford Literature Companions series follows the same approach and includes the following features:

- **Key quotations** from the novel
- **Key terms** explained on the page and linked to a complete glossary at the end of the book
- **Activity boxes** to help improve your understanding of the novel
- **UpGrade** tips to help prepare you for your exam

To help illustrate the features in this book, here are two annotated pages taken from this Oxford Literature Companion:

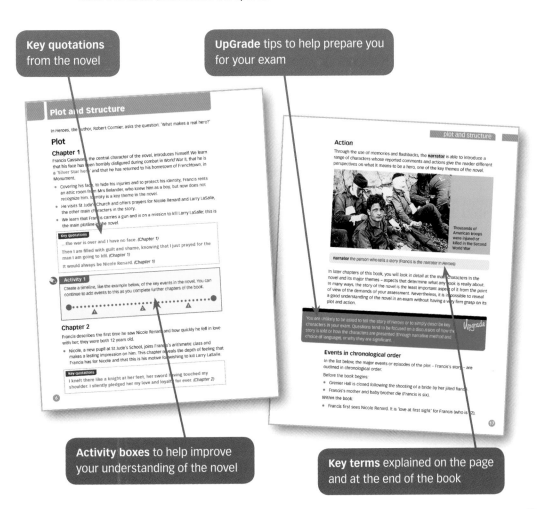

Key quotations from the novel

UpGrade tips to help prepare you for your exam

Activity boxes to help improve your understanding of the novel

Key terms explained on the page and at the end of the book

Plot and Structure

In *Heroes*, the author, Robert Cormier, asks the question: 'What makes a real hero?'

Plot

Chapter 1

Francis Cassavant, the central character of the novel, introduces himself. We learn that his face has been horribly disfigured during combat in World War II, that he is a **'Silver Star hero'** and that he has returned to his hometown of Frenchtown, in Monument.

- Covering his face, to hide his injuries and to protect his identity, Francis rents an attic room from Mrs Belander, who knew him as a boy, but now does not recognize him. Identity is a key theme in the novel.
- He visits St Jude's Church and offers prayers for Nicole Renard and Larry LaSalle, the other main characters in the story.
- We learn that Francis carries a gun and is on a mission to kill Larry LaSalle; this is the main plotline in the novel.

> **Key quotations**
>
> ...the war is over and I have no face. *(Chapter 1)*
>
> Then I am filled with guilt and shame, knowing that I just prayed for the man I am going to kill. *(Chapter 1)*
>
> It would always be Nicole Renard. *(Chapter 1)*

> **Activity 1**
>
> Create a timeline, like the example below, of the key events in the novel. You can continue to add events to this as you complete further chapters of the book.
>
>

Chapter 2

Francis describes the first time he saw Nicole Renard and how quickly he fell in love with her; they were both 12 years old.

- Nicole, a new pupil at St Jude's School, joins Francis's arithmetic class and makes a lasting impression on him. This chapter reveals the depth of feeling that Francis has for Nicole and that this is his motive for wishing to kill Larry LaSalle.

> **Key quotations**
>
> I knelt there like a knight at her feet, her sword having touched my shoulder. I silently pledged her my love and loyalty for ever. *(Chapter 2)*

Chapter 3

Francis felt like a knight worshipping his lady, rather like this 15th-century knight

Francis stands outside the house where Nicole used to live and recalls a conversation with a fellow Frenchtown soldier about her sudden disappearance from the town. He lies to Mrs Belander about his identity. We learn that Francis also forged his birth certificate to join the army, aged 15. Francis recounts his nightmare and remembers the horrors of war.

- Francis's feelings for Nicole are shown to be enduring and sincere.
- Francis's memories of the war reveal the unglamorous side of combat, underscoring the central concern of the novel about the nature of heroism.
- Francis describes how he killed two young German soldiers the day before the grenade 'blows my face away', emphasizing the senseless destruction of youth and innocence in the war.

Key quotations

...not like the war movies at the Plymouth, nobody displaying heroics or bravado. *(Chapter 3)*

...boys with apple cheeks, too young to shave. Like me. *(Chapter 3)*

Chapter 4

Francis meets Arthur Rivier, a former Frenchtown baseball hero, home from the war. Recognizing only a fellow **veteran**, Arthur takes Francis to the St Jude Club for a drink, where he meets many 'familiar faces' from before the war. Nobody recognizes Francis behind his scarf and cap as he listens to the veterans talk about their futures.

- We are introduced to a number of veterans whose lives, we will learn, have been damaged by the war.
- We hear them talk about heroes and heroism, the key theme of the novel.
- We are asked to think about 'faces' and how our faces help make us who we are.

veteran an experienced serviceman or woman who has served in the military forces; note that, while the term can also imply age (e.g. veteran cars), ironically the majority of veterans in *Heroes* are in their late teens or early twenties

Key quotations

I wanted to be like them, these heroes, fighting the Japs and the Germans... I was impatient to reach the age when I could join them in that great crusade for freedom. *(Chapter 4)*

I am not the hero he thinks I am, not like the other veterans here in the St Jude Club. *(Chapter 4)*

Chapter 5

Francis outlines the history of the Wreck Centre and the arrival of Larry LaSalle in Frenchtown. Francis's father has died and now Francis lives with his Uncle Louis. Out of loneliness, Francis joins the Wreck Centre where Larry is an inspirational leader. Nicole Renard joins the dancing group; she catches the attention of Larry and also makes Francis's 'life there complete'.

● The ominous history of the Wreck Centre is significant in introducing the themes of rivalry in love and revenge – themes that feature strongly in the main story.

● Larry's coaching and 'grooming' of the young people hints at more sinister intentions, which are revealed later in the plot.

Key quotations

"You are all stars," Larry LaSalle always told us. *(Chapter 5)*

In fact, the air of mystery that surrounded him added to his glamour. He was our champion and we were happy to be in his presence. *(Chapter 5)*

Chapter 6

Back at the St Jude Club, we meet the Strangler, the bartender, who keeps a scrapbook of 'Frenchtown warriors' and their achievements. Francis sees newspaper clippings celebrating Larry LaSalle's Silver Star and Arthur Rivier finally recognizes Francis, both as a Silver Star hero himself and as the 'champ' of the ping-pong table at the Wreck; but, at Francis's insistence, he promises, "I'll keep your secret."

● Themes of heroism, merit and gallantry are at the heart of this novel; Francis does not see himself as a hero, while others do.

● Francis reveals his identity (a key theme) unintentionally, when his own voice returns 'strong and clear' when he asks about his 'enemy' Larry LaSalle.

● The description of the veterans in this chapter, each damaged by the war in different ways, underlines the destructiveness of war.

"only the Silver Star is for heroism." *(Chapter 6)*

"You have your own Silver Star. You're in the Strangler's book, too." *(Chapter 6)*

"Little Francis Cassavant. Falls on a grenade and saves – how many men did you save, Francis?" *(Chapter 6)*

Chapter 7

Francis describes the table tennis championship at the Wreck. He recalls how Larry LaSalle boosted his confidence just as he 'groomed' other favourite girls and boys for a form of 'stardom'. Francis's continued adoration of Nicole was rewarded when she handed him the championship trophy after he beat Larry LaSalle, and she invited Francis to her party the following day.

- The theme of heroes, champions and stars is continued.
- The 'love' triangle between Francis, Nicole and Larry is symbolized through the table tennis competition and highlighted by Francis's **'agony of jealousy'** when Nicole calls Larry by his first name.
- The chapter ends with the shadow of war looming, since the 'tomorrow' that Nicole anticipates for her party is 7 December 1941, the date of the attack on Pearl Harbour.

Like a dream coming true, Nicole took the trophy from Larry LaSalle and handed it to me… *(Chapter 7)*

Two games were being played at the same time… *(Chapter 7)*

Chapter 8

Francis finds Arthur Rivier slumped in 'Pee Alley', very drunk and complaining that nobody talks about the war as it really was – **"the scared war"**. Francis confirms that **"Everybody was scared"** and Arthur scoffs at the very idea of the soldiers being heroes. Armand and Joe arrive and help Arthur home.

- The chapter directly addresses the theme of heroes and heroism and reveals that beneath their apparent good humour, the veterans are all damaged, either physically or psychologically, by the war.

"Nothing glamorous, like the write-ups in the papers or the newsreels. We weren't heroes. We were only there…" *(Chapter 8)*

Chapter 9

Larry LaSalle enlists in the fight against the 'Japs' and many others in Frenchtown follow his lead in a wave of **'patriotic fever'**. Nicole accepts Francis's invitation to the movies and their regular dates begin. News of Larry LaSalle's Silver Star reaches Frenchtown, confirmed by his appearance in the 'Movietone' news.

- The glorification of war, as seen at the movies and in newsreels, is contrasted with the reality of war as we saw it presented in Chapters 3 and 8.

- Francis appears to be genuinely happy for the first time in the novel as his innocent and loving relationship with Nicole blossoms. They consider their futures as a writer (Francis) and nurse (Nicole) in an optimistic way, neither knowing what is actually in store for them.

> **Key quotations**
>
> **Every day, page five of the *Times* carried stories and pictures of our fighting forces, often announcing medals awarded for valour on the battlefields.** *(Chapter 9)*
>
> **We had discovered in one moment on a Sunday afternoon that the world was not a safe place any more.** *(Chapter 9)*

Chapter 10

Francis remembers the first time he saw his disfigured face when he was in London. His friend, Enrico, gives him an 'aviator's' white scarf to conceal his injuries. Francis tells us he is now closing **'doors to the future'** by burning the addresses of Dr Abrams, who could help him, and of hospitals where he might find his friend Enrico again.

Francis and Nicole enjoyed Saturday matinees at the cinema, which were popular long before television

- Francis's face is highly significant as the novel deals with issues of identity, disguise and disfigurement.

- Francis's future is dominated by thoughts of his 'mission' and then his own 'disposal', a word that betrays Francis's lack of self-worth.

Activity 2

Faces are important in this novel. As you read, make a note of all the references to facial features that you can find.

Chapter 11

Larry LaSalle returns to a hero's welcome as Monument celebrates his Silver Star. He surprises the Wreck Centre gang by re-opening the Centre for one night of dancing and table tennis. Later, Francis disregards Larry's instruction to go home and, instead, waits for Nicole in the foyer while Larry has **'one last dance'** alone with her. When he realizes that Larry is assaulting Nicole, Francis is powerless to intervene. Nicole runs away from Larry but, when she sees Francis, shoots him a look that shows she feels betrayed by him.

- This crucial chapter reveals Francis's motive for his mission to kill Larry LaSalle.
- Larry's rapturous welcome home contrasts starkly with Francis's own 'anonymous' return.
- Larry's nonchalant 'whistling' of *Dancing in the Dark* reveals the sinister side of a man who, up to this point, has been presented in a positive light. His encouragement of the 'Wreck Centre gang' has been exposed as a systematic 'grooming' of the young people in his care, for his own ends.
- Francis's inability to protect Nicole leaves Francis wracked with guilt, another key theme.

Key quotations

I recognized in her eyes now what I could not deny: betrayal. My betrayal of her in her eyes. *(Chapter 11)*

It's amazing that the heart makes no noise when it cracks. *(Chapter 11)*

Chapter 12

Francis describes the agony of waiting to talk to Nicole after the assault; she blames him for his inaction and tells him to go away. In despair, Francis climbs to the steeple of St Jude's Church, determined to kill himself. Suddenly realizing that committing suicide would disgrace his family name, he decides instead to join the army where he could die **'with honour'**.

- The chapter reveals Francis's burden of guilt at having 'betrayed' Nicole.
- Francis's rejection of suicide as a way out shows how his religion affects his actions; his concern for his family name continues the theme of identity.

> **Key quotations**
>
> I could only stand there mute, as if all my sins had been revealed and there was no forgiveness for them. *(Chapter 12)*
>
> Soldiers were dying with honour on battlefields all over the world. Noble deaths. The deaths of heroes. How could I die by leaping from a steeple? *(Chapter 12)*

Chapters 13 and 14

Francis overhears a conversation between Mrs Belander and her neighbour, which reveals that Larry LaSalle has returned. Determined to carry out his 'mission', Francis takes his gun and goes straight to the tenement where Larry is living. Francis announces his identity but is taken aback by Larry's warm reception of him.

Francis confronts Larry about the rape of Nicole and reveals that this is the reason why he wanted to die. He takes out his gun, but Larry reveals his own gun and his intention to kill himself, telling Francis, **"you've accomplished your mission here"** *(Chapter 14)*. As Francis leaves, he hears the pistol shot that ends Larry's life.

- Chapter 14 is the **climax** of the novel and ends Francis's mission. Larry asks a very important question of Francis: **"Does that one sin of mine wipe away all the good things?"** *(Chapter 14)*
- Larry kills himself in an act of **atonement**, which saves Francis from having to commit the **mortal sin** of murder. This religious concept is very significant to the themes of guilt and forgiveness that are prominent in the novel.

> **Key quotations**
>
> The sound of a pistol shot cracks the air... The sound from this distance is almost like that of a ping-pong ball striking the table. *(Chapter 14)*

atonement something that is done to make amends for a wrong action; it is supposed to help to 'wipe away' a sin

climax a turning point in the action of a novel; the moment where the action or crisis reaches its greatest intensity

mortal sin in the Catholic church, a sin that condemns the sinner to Hell

Chapter 15

Francis visits the convent, where Sister Mathilde gives him the address of Nicole's new school in Albany. Before he leaves, he tells Sister Mathilde about the doctor who has promised to fix up his face.

- Although Francis claims to the reader that this is a lie, we have a strong impression that Francis is moving towards a new future here.

> **Key quotations**
>
> "I'll be as good as new…" *(Chapter 15)*

Chapter 16

Francis visits Nicole, but they do not recognize each other immediately. They reminisce about the past. Nicole apologizes for having blamed Francis for what Larry did to her. When Nicole calls Francis, **"My good Francis […] My Silver Star hero"** Francis admits he no longer knows what a hero is. Her words of encouragement, **"Write about it, Francis. Maybe you can find an answer that way"**, seem to act as a spur to Francis. Nicole kisses him goodbye.

- A reader expecting a traditional happy ending will be disappointed. Nicole's parting words have an air of finality about them, **"Have a good life, Francis. Be whatever will make you happy."** Nevertheless, these words have the promise of a future for Francis.
- Themes of forgiveness, identity and loss are central to this chapter.

> **Key quotations**
>
> "Now I'm starting to find out what I am, who I really am…" *(Chapter 16)*
>
> ''I don't know what a hero is any more, Nicole." I think of Larry LaSalle and his Silver Star. And my own Silver Star, for an act of cowardice. *(Chapter 16)*

Chapter 17

At the station, Francis watches people coming and going. He reflects on his conversation with Nicole and suddenly realizes that the heroes were the ordinary soldiers like those in his platoon. That momentous insight, perhaps, convinces him of his own worth and he considers his options for the future – maybe to write, to find Dr Abrams and Enrico. Having made the decision, 'I should do all those things', he picks up his duffel bag and heads 'for the exit and the next train to leave the station'.

The Silver Star, the third highest US decoration awarded for bravery in combat, is still awarded today

- Francis thinks about the gun in his bag, as well as about contacting Dr Abrams and Enrico, and it is possible to conclude that he has not stopped wanting to die. However, we are reading the book that tells us his story and the implication is, of course, that Francis became a writer.

> **Key quotations**
>
> *We were only there*. Scared kids, not born to fight or kill. Who were not only there but who stayed, did not run away, fought the good war. And never talk about it. And didn't receive a Silver Star. But heroes, anyway. The real heroes. *(Chapter 17)*

Structure

The structure of a novel is determined by the order in which the story is told, as well as by the ways in which different points of view are presented within it. The structure is the result of careful shaping by the author, who must initially engage the reader's attention while introducing aspects of character, plot and theme; the author must then maintain the reader's interest while the plot develops to a climax, crisis or key event, and then lead the reader to a satisfying conclusion.

Narrative viewpoint

Heroes is written in the **first person**, as if by Francis, who confides in us about his life. As readers, we build up a clear picture of Francis and sympathize with him as he tells us his gripping story.

chronological narrative the presentation of events in a story in the order in which they actually occurred

first-person narration a story told from the narrator's point of view, using the pronouns 'I' or 'me'

flashback a sudden recollection of a previous event that shifts the action back into the past

memory the recollection of a past event *in the present*; the action is not transported back to the past, although memories give the reader an insight into Francis's past experiences

narrative structure the way in which a writer organizes a story to create meaning

narrative technique a method that a novelist uses to tell his or her story

Time

Some of the chapters in *Heroes* deal with events from Francis's past, when he was in his early teen years or, later, when he was a soldier. These chapters are written in the past tense.

Other chapters deal with Francis's life in the present. Here the author uses the present tense and the events that are described appear to be happening in the here and now.

Some of the longer chapters contain both present and past events and, at times, the past and the present appear almost to merge together. Rarely, but significantly, Francis considers his future.

The story is not told in **chronological order** but appears as a description of present-day events, punctuated by **memories** and **flashbacks**. Remember, too, that even the present-day action is set in 1945.

Cormier's complicated use of time is a critical **narrative technique**, which enables him to build up quite a detailed picture of his characters in a relatively short novel. The story moves both backward and forward in time and also back and forth amongst Francis's memories, picking out those moments that best reveal aspects of each character's personality or which help to illuminate the novel's key themes.

This use of time contributes to the **narrative structure** of the novel, which begins with Francis's arrival in Frenchtown to confront his past and ends with his departure from the railway station in Albany, to begin his future.

Cormier shapes the novel by arranging his chapters in such a way that the memories of the past and the descriptions of the present merge almost seamlessly, fitting together like pieces of a jigsaw puzzle until we finally understand Francis's motive for wanting to kill Larry LaSalle.

Below is a table that shows which time frame Cormier is using in each chapter.

Chapter	Time frame in the chapters
1	Mainly set in the **present**, this chapter deals with Francis's return to Frenchtown with a number of **memories** of characters from Francis's **past**.
2	Set entirely in the **past**, this chapter describes the arrival of Nicole in Francis's life and his feelings for her. The whole chapter is a **flashback**.
3	This chapter begins and ends in the **present**, in Frenchtown, but contains two significant **flashbacks** to Francis's experiences in the war.
4	Set entirely in the present, although Francis meets familiar faces from before the war. He also hears music that **reminds** him of the English hospital in his **past**.
5	This chapter begins and ends in the **present**. Francis describes the history of the Wreck Centre before slipping into a lengthy **flashback** about the role of Larry LaSalle.
6	This is set in the **present** throughout at the bar of the St Jude Club, although the conversation is largely about the **past**.
7	This is set in the **past** and presented as a **flashback**. Francis describes the table tennis championship. The chapter closes with Nicole's party invitation for '**tomorrow**'.
8	Set in the **present**, Francis describes meeting Arthur Rivier who is drunk and depressed.
9	Set entirely in the **past**, this chapter consists of three main **flashbacks**: Larry LaSalle's decision to enlist; Francis's invitation to Nicole for a 'date'; and news of Larry's Silver Star.
10	This chapter begins in the **past** with a **flashback** to England and then shifts to the **present**. Although Francis says he is closing 'doors to the future', he **anticipates** the 'second home-coming' of Larry La Salle before lapsing into a **memory** of the first.

Chapter	Time frame in the chapters
11	Set in the **past** and told entirely in **flashback**, this critical chapter describes the events of Larry's home-coming, the celebration of his 'bravery' and his cowardly rape of Nicole.
12	Set in the **past**, Francis describes his sense of guilt. His conversation with Nicole and his thoughts about suicide and dying an honourable death are related in **flashback**.
13	This brief chapter returns to the **present** and Francis discovers exactly where he can find Larry LaSalle.
14	This chapter is set in the **present** although it contains several **memories**. Francis describes his final, fatal encounter with Larry LaSalle.
15	Set in the **present**, Francis visits the convent, where Sister Mathilde gives him Nicole's address. There is a sense of the **future** in his anticipated reunion with Nicole.
16	This is set in the **present** in Nicole's new school. Francis and Nicole **reminisce** about the **past** and talk about their separate potential '**futures**', hers as a teacher and his as a writer.
17	The final chapter is set in the **present** at the railroad station. Francis **reflects** on his talk with Nicole and seems to make a decision to move forward into his **future**.

Place

In addition to moving between the past and the present, the action of the novel also moves between different locations.

- Frenchtown in Monument. This is the district of Monument where Francis grew up and where he returns to after the war. Within Frenchtown are:
  - Francis's school, St Jude's Parochial School (**past**)
  - The Wreck Centre (**past** and **present**)
  - Mrs Belander's tenement apartment (**present**)
  - At home with father/uncle (**past**) in a house on Fifth Street
  - The streets of Frenchtown (**past** and **present**)
  - Nicole's three-decker house (**past** and **present**)
  - Mr Laurier's store (**past**)
  - The St Jude Club (**present**)
  - St Jude's Church (**past** and **present**)
  - The convent (**past** and **present**)
  - City hall (**past**)
- French villages (**past**)
- Hospitals in France and England (**past**)
- Nicole's school in Albany (**present**)
- The railroad station (**present**)

Activity 3

Create your own table showing the location(s) of the action of the novel, chapter by chapter.

Action

Through the use of memories and flashbacks, the **narrator** is able to introduce a range of characters whose reported comments and actions give the reader different perspectives on what it means to be a hero, one of the key themes of the novel.

Thousands of American troops were injured or killed in the Second World War

narrator the person who tells a story (Francis is the narrator in *Heroes*)

In later chapters of this book, you will look in detail at the main characters in the novel and its major themes – aspects that determine what any book is really about. In many ways, the story of the novel is the least important aspect of it from the point of view of the demands of your assessment. Nevertheless, it is impossible to reveal a good understanding of the novel in an exam without having a very firm grasp on its plot and action.

You are unlikely to be asked to tell the story of *Heroes* or to simply describe key characters in your exam. Questions tend to be focused on a discussion of how the story is told or how the characters are presented (through narrative method and choice of language), or why they are significant.

Events in chronological order

In the list below, the major events or episodes of the plot – Francis's story – are outlined in chronological order.

Before the book begins:

- Grenier Hall is closed following the shooting of a bride by her jilted fiancé.
- Francis's mother and baby brother die (Francis is six).

Within the book:

- Francis first sees Nicole Renard. It is 'love at first sight' for Francis (who is 12).

- After Francis tells Marie LaCroix that he likes Nicole, Nicole speaks and later waves to him.
- Francis wins Sister Mathilde's 'medal' for composition at around this time.
- The Wreck Centre is opened by Larry LaSalle. Francis takes up calisthenics.
- Francis's father dies and Francis is taken in by his Uncle Louis. Mrs Belander bakes Francis a birthday cake (he is 13).
- Encouraged by Larry LaSalle to play table tennis, Francis becomes table tennis champion at the Wreck Centre. Nicole presents him with a trophy and invites him to her party.
- The USA declares war on Japan following Japan's attack on Pearl Harbour.
- Larry LaSalle announces his intention to enlist in the war. The Wreck Centre closes.
- Francis takes a job at Laurier's Store, after school. Nicole comes in to buy sweets, they discuss books and films; Francis plucks up the courage to ask Nicole on a date.
- Francis and Nicole begin dating; she allows him to kiss her innocently in the cinema.
- News comes that Larry LaSalle has been awarded the Silver Star for gallantry.
- Larry LaSalle returns, on leave, to a hero's welcome. He lures the young people to the Wreck Centre, where he rapes Nicole. Francis overhears what is happening but is unable to act or save her.
- Nicole accuses Francis of having let her down.
- Larry LaSalle disappears from Frenchtown the day after the rape.
- Francis feels so guilty about what happened to Nicole that he considers, but rejects, suicide; instead, he alters his birth certificate in order to join the army (he is 14 or 15).
- Francis's platoon is deployed to France.
- Nicole goes to Francis's home to apologize for blaming him about what happened with Larry. She is too late as he has enlisted.
- Uncle Louis returns to Canada.
- Francis meets Norman Rocheleau in a French village; Norman tells him that Nicole has moved away from Frenchtown.
- Francis kills two German soldiers in self-defence and the next day jumps on a grenade, saving the lives of numerous comrades but losing most of his face.
- Francis is treated, first in France and then in a hospital in England. He meets Dr Abrams, who helps to repair his face a little and who promises further treatment after the war.
- Francis meets Enrico Rucelli, who was maimed in the war. They talk about Nicole.
- Francis goes to London on a three-day pass and discovers the extent of his injuries as passers-by turn away from him. Enrico gives him a white aviator's scarf and Francis adopts it as part of his 'cover-up' strategy.
- Francis returns to Frenchtown. The war is over. He has money and a gun in his duffel bag but he has no face, only a mission to kill Larry LaSalle.
- Francis rents a room from Mrs Belander without revealing his identity. For a while, nobody recognizes him.

- He visits St Jude's Church to pray.
- He meets Arthur Rivier, who invites him for a drink in the St Jude Club, which is full of ex-servicemen.
- Francis finds Arthur, drunk, in an alley one night and Arthur scoffs at the notion of heroes.
- Francis hears that Larry LaSalle has returned to Frenchtown and goes to confront him.
- Larry welcomes Francis like an old friend and tries to make him feel good about himself again as a hero, whose disfigured face is a badge of honour.
- Francis confesses that he wanted to die because of what Larry did to Nicole. He produces his gun and tells Larry to say his prayers.
- Larry has his own gun and admits that he has thought of killing himself. He shows no remorse for exploiting 'the sweet young things' but is disturbed by Francis's reaction to his sin and asks: **"Does that one sin of mine wipe away all the good things?"** *(Chapter 14)* He begs Francis to leave and to leave all the bad things behind with him.
- Francis leaves and Larry LaSalle shoots himself.
- Francis visits the convent where Sister Mathilde gives him Nicole's address in Albany.
- Francis visits Nicole, hoping that she will still be his 'girl', but she is changed both physically and mentally. She apologizes for how she blamed him after the rape.
- Nicole encourages Francis to write down his story to help to make sense of the war and of his ideas about heroes; her parting kiss and the words **"Have a good life, Francis. Be whatever makes you happy"** *(Chapter 16)* effectively end the relationship.
- Francis leaves to board the next train and begin the rest of his life.

Activity 4

1. Rearrange the events listed above into four separate lists according to which you think are the most significant events in terms of the novel's meaning (i.e. what the author is trying to communicate to his readers through plot, characters, context, themes and choice of language). Head your lists: Most significant, Very significant, Fairly significant and Fairly insignificant. You do not have to have the same number of points in each list.

2. Go back through the book and find out in which chapter each of the events listed occurs. This will help you to see the complex way in which Cormier crafts the plot.

Writing about the plot and structure

Upgrade

In your assessment, you are likely to need to refer to the plot of *Heroes*, as well as the narrative viewpoint and the author's use of time and place in the structure of the novel. Remember to keep your answer focused on the question and use quotations for evidence.

Biography of Robert Cormier

- Robert Cormier was born in Leominster, Massachusetts, USA in 1925 and he grew up in the French–Canadian neighbourhood of French Hill. He was raised as a Catholic and, during his early years, was educated by nuns.

- He was 16 years old in 1941 when the Japanese attack on Pearl Harbour brought America into the Second World War, which had started in Europe in 1939.

- Robert Cormier did not serve in the war because of his poor eyesight. Instead, having studied first at Leominster School and then at Fitchburg State College, he began working as a journalist for a local newspaper.

- Cormier worked as a journalist for 30 years and lived in French Hill all of his life. Towards the end of his career as a newspaper man, he published his first novel for young adults, *The Chocolate War*, a novel that dealt with the themes of intimidation and peer pressure.

- Cormier's literary influences include Ernest Hemingway, Jack London, Graham Greene and F. Scott Fitzgerald – all great writers of the first half of the 20th century.

- Cormier's novels are also influenced by the cinema. He grew up in what many consider to be the 'golden age of movies' and some of his narrative techniques have been described by critics as being more filmic than literary.

- From 1974 to his death in 2000, Cormier wrote 19 books, most of which have been described as books for young adults. Many of these are set in and around Frenchtown, the name that Cormier gave to his own neighbourhood in Leominster, which provided him with the inspiration for his stories.

- Robert Cormier won many awards for his writing of fiction for young adults.

- *Heroes* was published in 1998. It has been said that Robert Cormier was inspired to write *Heroes* by the 50th anniversary celebrations of the D-Day landings. At this time, the stories of many veterans of the Second World War were told or retold and acts of their heroism were regularly discussed in the media.

Activity 1

Re-read the biographical points about Robert Cormier's life. Identify those aspects of his life that appear to have influenced the writing of *Heroes*.

Historical and cultural context of the novel

The Second World War and its aftermath

There is no need to go into detail here about the history of the Second World War, a war fought across several continents, over a six-year period, which was responsible for the death or injury of millions of soldiers and civilians on both 'sides' of the conflict. However, America's involvement in the Second World War, and the impact that the war had upon the characters in *Heroes*, is absolutely central both to the plot of the novel and to one of its recurring themes – the nature of heroism.

Despite the fact that the war between Germany and Britain, along with their European and Commonwealth allies, had been raging since 1939, many people in America believed that it would be bad for the United States, politically and financially, to be drawn into a conflict that appeared to be essentially a European problem. That all changed when the Japanese attacked Pearl Harbour – an American naval base in Hawaii – on 7 December 1941, killing over 2500 Americans. The shock of the Japanese **'sneak attack'** *(Chapter 9)* (as it is described in *Heroes*) changed public opinion in America overnight and created a tide of patriotism that resulted in many young men rushing to enlist into the armed forces.

'With war undeclared, Japan attacked Pearl Harbour. American Isolationism died in the raid...'

When the Japanese attacked Pearl Harbour, Robert Cormier was about the same age as Francis Cassavant is in *Heroes* when war is declared. The description of the impact of the war on an ordinary community in the novel is clearly a historically accurate one. Cormier writes about:

- **'fathers and brothers'** *(Chapter 9)* joining the armed forces
- local factories (like the 'comb shop') joining the war effort, working round the clock and perhaps manufacturing **'secret material in a special section of the factory'** *(Chapter 9)* for the war effort
- women taking over the jobs of the young men who had joined the services and even becoming uniformed personnel themselves: **'They were called Waves and Spars and walked the streets with a pride in their step'** *(Chapter 9)*.

Cormier's descriptions of the ways in which Frenchtown reacted to the war are clearly based on historical facts observed first hand by the author.

Cormier did not have first-hand experience of combat, however, and in the novel he gives us only brief glimpses of life on the battlefield. In *Heroes*, Larry LaSalle **'was one of the first Frenchtown men to enlist in the armed services'** *(Chapter 9)*. Larry becomes a marine whose platoon was deployed in the Pacific, while Francis becomes a soldier whose company was sent to Europe. Francis's company were stationed in France, where American soldiers joined with their British and other Commonwealth and European allies in a mission to defeat the Germans and their allies. Cormier does not dwell on the war-time action of either of these key characters in any detail except in his brief narration of Francis's 'nightmare' experience of killing the two German soldiers in Chapter 3 and in Nicole's even briefer report of the act of 'heroism' that earned Larry LaSalle his Silver Star: **"He saved the lives of an entire platoon [...] Captured an enemy machine gun nest"** *(Chapter 9)*.

Other war exploits are only vaguely mentioned and generally involve death (**'poor Joey LeBlanc, who died on a beach on Iwo Jima'** *(Chapter 5)*), injury (**'Henry Johnson wounded, his chest ripped open by shrapnel'** *(Chapter 3)*), or sheer terror (**"the boys of Frenchtown. Scared and homesick and cramps in the stomach and vomit"** *(Chapter 8)*).

Cormier certainly does not glamorize war, but deals mostly with its 'after effects'. For example, despite describing Larry's first home-coming (where he returns on leave with his Silver Star) as being a hero's welcome, Cormier also shows that his second home-coming attracts only Francis's attention. Larry's dancing days are over: **'jungle fever'** *(Chapter 14)* has claimed him and he is simply **'worn out'** *(Chapter 14)*. Through Larry and Francis, Arthur, George Richelieu and the other veterans at the St Jude Club, Cormier shows how thousands upon thousands of real-life veterans returned to their home towns with horrific injuries, mental or physical, as the war came to an end. Little wonder then that the words **'adjust to his condition'** *(Chapter 1)*, which Francis includes in his prayers for Enrico Rucelli (who lost both legs and one arm in the fighting), are described by Francis as **'terrible words'** *(Chapter 1)* since the conditions that these veterans had to adjust to were, indeed, often terrible. Robert Cormier documents their difficulties in adjusting to post-war life in *Heroes*, especially in the chapters set in the St Jude Club (Chapters 4, 6 and 8).

The St Jude Club is one place where the veterans meet when they return from the war. Isolated from their former friends and family by their horrific experiences, the veterans form a new 'brotherhood' within the wider community of Frenchtown and Monument. Francis describes this as **'a camaraderie in the bar, a fellowship that I wish I could be a part of'** *(Chapter 4)*. Ironically, however, as Arthur complains in Chapter 8, **"Nobody talks about the war"**. Instead, the veterans talk about growing up in Frenchtown before the war, discuss the GI Bill and plan their futures.

The GI Bill, also called the 'Serviceman's Readjustment Act' was intended to help those servicemen returning from the war to reintegrate into civilian life. In addition to making sure that soldiers received generous 'mustering out' pay when they left the services (remember Francis has **'plenty of money'** *(Chapter 1)*), President

Roosevelt's government pledged to pay for higher education for all ex-servicemen and women if they wanted to pursue it (the route Joe LaFontaine intends to take and the one that Francis talks to Nicole about taking at their final meeting). In Chapter 6, Cormier shows us very clearly how fragile and damaged some of these veterans were. The bill was signed by President Roosevelt in 1944 and he stated his intention that it would give 'emphatic notice to the men and women in our armed forces that the American people do not intend to let them down'. There is an implication here that Roosevelt, and indeed all Americans, regarded the returning veterans as 'heroes'.

Activity 2

Each time you re-read a chapter of the novel, make a note of the number of times that the words 'hero' and 'heroes' appear. You will soon be in double figures! Try to work out, each time, how the word(s) are being used. Are they always used to refer specifically to heroism in war? What other types of hero are there in the novel? Who are your heroes and why?

It is also worth noting that while the action of this novel is clearly set in the 1930s and 1940s, and relates to action during and after the Second World War, Robert Cormier lived through several more modern conflicts, including the Korean War, the Vietnam War and the First Gulf War, before writing *Heroes*. Each of these wars involved American forces and each brought danger, disfigurement or death to thousands of American servicemen and women. Cormier's investigation in *Heroes* into what makes a real 'hero' is relevant to every generation that is affected by conflict and every nation that sees its armed forces go to war. Cormier uses the Second World War to ask questions about all wars and about what heroism might mean today, as well as in the early part of the 20th century.

The courtly love tradition

Heroes is not just about war or revenge, of course. At its heart there is a love story – the love story of Francis and Nicole Renard. This love story is depicted in a very specific way by Robert Cormier, using **allusions** throughout to a traditional form of 'Romance' literature that dates back to medieval times and deals with a particular type of love known as 'courtly love'.

allusion (in literature) a reference to other literary texts such as plays, poems or novels or to specific literary traditions

Courtly love describes a relationship that is based on the feudal relationship between a knight and his king. The knight serves his courtly lady with the same obedience and loyalty that he owes to his sovereign. Within this tradition, the lady is in complete control of the relationship, while the knight owes her obedience and submission. The knight's love for the lady inspires him to do great deeds, in order to be worthy of her love or to win her favour.

The features of courtly love include the following elements:

- The love is between a deserving and noble-minded man (often a knight, in tales of chivalry) and an unattainable and beautiful lady (or damsel).
- Love, on the part of the knight, is immediate and at first sight; it is enduring love that never dies.
- The love is often secret.
- The love is chaste but passionately felt.
- The knight reveres, respects and adores the lady with an almost religious devotion.
- The knight experiences a mixture of agony and ecstasy in his love for the lady.
- The knight looks for opportunities to serve the lady and is willing to undergo ordeals for the sake of his lady.
- The lady occasionally rewards her knight with a 'favour', which might be a handkerchief, a scarf or other trophy.

Activity 3

Write down examples of these features of courtly love that are referred to in the descriptions of the relationship between Francis and Nicole.

Chapter 2 describes the first time that Francis saw Nicole. Cormier alludes to courtly love here to show that Francis is ready to idolize Nicole, just as a courtly lover might idolize his unattainable lady. When Nicole enters the school room, Francis is already kneeling and he describes her as **'the most beautiful girl I had ever seen'** *(Chapter 2)*. He also compares her to the statue of St Thérèse because of the **'pale purity'** *(Chapter 2)* of her face and confides that **'I knelt there like a knight at her feet, her sword having touched my shoulder. I silently pledged her love and loyalty for ever'** *(Chapter 2)*.

By using the language of chivalry throughout Chapter 2 – 'knight', 'sword', 'pledge', 'vow' and 'agony' – Cormier is drawing attention to the courtly love tradition whereby the knight sees himself in the service of his beloved. This idea is continued when Francis explains how he wished that Nicole might drop one of her books so that he could be of service to her (**'rush forward and pick it up'** *(Chapter 2)*) and when he explains that he wants to shout from the rooftops, **"I love her with all my heart"** *(Chapter 2)*. Francis describes himself waiting for Nicole to appear **'Standing [...] in an agony of love and longing, like a sentry on lonely guard duty'** *(Chapter 2)*. In this sentence, Cormier blends ideas of courtly love with military service. Nicole's presence has a physical effect on Francis, whose **'mouth would instantly dry up'** *(Chapter 2)* yet still **'vowing to talk to her the next time'** *(Chapter 1)*.

Lancelot proves his love for Guinevere by crossing a river and rescuing her from a tower, 14th century

Francis's increasing 'courtly' devotion to Nicole is also emphasized in Chapter 5, where even her perspiration is adored and idealized by Francis, who describes the drops like **'raindrops on white porcelain'** *(Chapter 5)*. He admits that Nicole's presence at the Wreck Centre, **'made my life there complete'** *(Chapter 5)*. Francis also alludes to his **'secret love'** *(Chapter 7)* for Nicole when he is speculating about Larry LaSalle's favouritism of the pair of them. This chapter is also important in revealing Francis's jealousy of Larry when Nicole refers to him using his first name only. She does this when she is inviting Francis to her party, an invitation that causes him both **'delight and agony'** *(Chapter 7)*; these are the typical contrasting emotions of the courtly lover, whose love both ennobles (makes him a better person) and pains him.

Francis's joy in winning the table tennis championship is enhanced by being awarded the trophy – another key word in the courtly love vocabulary – by Nicole. She had already favoured him by blowing him a lady-like kiss of encouragement. Francis is amazed and gratified when Nicole whispers **"my champion"** *(Chapter 7)* in his ear and he sees **'her joyous face, hands joined together, as if in prayer […] as if making herself an offering to me'** *(Chapter 7)*. This is perhaps the happiest moment of Francis's life, as described in the novel.

When Francis and Nicole begin dating, Francis can hardly believe his good fortune. When he asks her if she would like to go to a movie with him, he feels that her reply is so important to him that **'The earth paused in its orbit'** *(Chapter 9)*. Even the kisses that they share in the movie theatre are innocent and, despite Francis's clear sexual attraction to Nicole, his respect and reverence for her is evident throughout.

It is because of Francis's pure love for Nicole that he is so distraught by her unspoken accusation of betrayal after the rape in Chapter 11. Nicole seems wary of being left alone with Larry. Although Francis had assured her, earlier in the chapter, that **"I'll never leave you"** *(Chapter 11)*, pressured by Larry's insistence Francis does begin to leave. However, in another echo of the courtly love tradition, rather than leaving, Francis stations himself **'in the small foyer'** *(Chapter 11)*; he anticipates the moment when the dancing is over and he will be able to tell his 'lady' that: **'I had stayed, would never desert her, that she had told me not to go and I hadn't, that she was more important to me than Larry LaSalle'** *(Chapter 11)*.

Rather than being taken as a 'service' by Nicole, the fact that Francis overheard her being raped and did nothing to prevent it seems to her to be an act of betrayal. It is Francis's realization of this that convinces him that he should end his life. It is possible to see his quest for death as part of his continued attempt to serve his 'lady', Nicole.

When Francis finally finds Nicole at her new school in Albany at the end of the novel, there are more allusions to courtly love. There is no conventional 'happy ending' for the pair. Nicole's gentle kiss is a farewell, although she still calls him **"My good Francis. My table tennis champion. My Silver Star hero..."** *(Chapter 16)*. Nicole's encouragement to him to write about his experiences, **"I always thought you'd be a writer"** *(Chapter 16)* and her command to **"Write about it, Francis"** *(Chapter 16)* gives him a renewed sense of purpose, another 'service' that he can perform for her. Her parting words, **"Have a good life, Francis. Be whatever will make you happy"** *(Chapter 16)*, demonstrate how the knight's love for the 'unattainable' lady can better his life.

When writing about Cormier's use of the courtly love tradition within the novel, make sure that you offer several specific textual examples, drawn from different parts of the novel, to support your ideas.

The Catholic Church

The community of Frenchtown in Monument is a relatively poor one, but it is evidently a close-knit community centred on the Catholic Church of St Jude's parish. The steeple of St Jude's is referred to on numerous occasions and seems to be a highly visible 'landmark' for Francis. The majority of those who live in Frenchtown are Catholic. They attend St Jude's Church for worship and send their children to St Jude's Parochial School, where the teachers are nuns.

In the Catholic Church, St Jude is the patron saint of 'lost causes'. A 'patron saint' is a saint who is considered to be a special guardian to a specific group of people, for example, in a trade or profession or to a specific country.

Cormier's novel contains many references to St Jude's Church, the convent and the school that Francis and Nicole attend. Sisters Mathilde, Gertrude and Perpetua, to name but three, are amongst the influential characters in Francis's life and Father Balthazar is mentioned on a number of occasions. Francis also tells us that he was once an altar boy. The religious context of the novel is emphatically Catholic and there are numerous mentions of Catholic prayers and rituals throughout. Sin and forgiveness are recurrent themes.

One of Francis's first actions on returning to Frenchtown in Chapter 1 is to visit the church to pray for Enrico, for the souls of his mother and father, for Nicole Renard and finally for his 'enemy', Larry LaSalle. Later in the novel, we learn that it is because of Francis's faith in the Catholic Church's teachings about suicide that he decides not to kill himself by jumping from the steeple of St Jude's, despite his self-loathing and guilt about what happened to Nicole. He chooses to enlist and seek death in battle, rather than disgrace his family name. In the Catholic faith, suicide is regarded as a sin. However, someone who dies in the act of saving the lives of others is not considered to be sinful, as self-sacrifice is a virtue.

Throughout the novel, Cormier often uses vocabulary that has religious **connotations**. One of the most important of these terms is 'mission', which Cormier uses to describe Francis's plan to kill Larry LaSalle. In a religious context, missionaries are individuals or groups of people sent by the Church to foreign lands on a 'mission' to spread the faith and to save souls. Francis's 'mission' is a blend of both the military and the religious; he plans to shoot Larry with the gun he has brought from the war and, in doing so, eliminate someone that he sees as a 'sinner'. Larry, too, seems to understand the religious nature of Francis's murderous intention. In Chapter 14, at the climax of the novel when Francis finally confronts Larry about his sin, Larry begs Francis to put down his gun and to: **"Leave everything here, the war, what happened at the Wreck Centre, leave it all behind, with me"** *(Chapter 14)*. He assures Francis that **"Whether you know it or not, you've accomplished your mission here"** *(Chapter 14)*, because Larry has taken the decision to shoot himself and he does not want Francis's soul charged with the mortal sin of murder.

> **connotation** an association created by a word – not its actual meaning, but ideas or qualities it implies
>
> **furlough** approved time off from military service

Activity 4

Re-read Chapters 12, 14 and 15. Make a list of every reference you can find that seems to be linked to combat, religion or the courtly love tradition. How do these repeated references affect our perceptions about Francis?

Youth culture

Heroes is concerned mainly with young people. It covers the period of Francis's life from when he is 12 to 18 years of age. In that time he grows up alongside the youth of Frenchtown, fellow pupils at St Jude's Parochial School, fellow members of the Wreck Centre and fellow fresh-faced soldiers in the army.

We are given an insight into what school was like for Francis (and for Joey LeBlanc) with the nuns as teachers. Cormier describes Francis's friendship with Marie LaCroix and Joey LeBlanc, and outlines the activities at the Wreck Centre, the dancing and singing, the callisthenics and the table tennis championship. When Francis and Nicole start dating, they become regulars at the Plymouth Theatre where they watch movies and cowboy serials; they share a taste for **'Butterscotch bits'** *(Chapter 9)* and **'Milk Duds'** *(Chapter 9)*. When Larry returns on **furlough**, we hear about how

Nicole and Marie **'jitterbugged'** *(Chapter 12)* at the Wreck and about the young people's pleasure at finding **'soda pop and candy bars'** *(Chapter 12)*. After the war, Francis socializes with the young veterans at the St Jude Club and he mentions the music playing on the juke-box.

In the 1940s, jitterbug was danced to swing music

Cormier records the pleasures and challenges of being young in small-town America, in Francis's matter-of-fact and unemotional voice. When you are writing about the context of the novel in your exam, remember to mention that although Cormier does write about adults in the novel, he focuses on their interaction with the young people and especially with Francis and Nicole; the novel is primarily about the young.

Writing about context

Upgrade

In your assessment, you may need to refer to the aspects of pre- and post-war American culture covered in this chapter in your answers to the questions set, for example:

- The novel's setting in a small community in the time leading up to and immediately after the war provides its immediate context.

- The use of typically American words and phrases as well as Cormier's treatment of youth culture.

- How this novel, set in post-war America, is still relevant today.

- The French–Canadian influence, which is demonstrated very clearly in the names of the characters.

Characters

There are three main characters in the novel: Francis Cassavant, Nicole Renard and Larry LaSalle. Francis is the most important character, as it is his experience and his thoughts that make up the substance of the book. Nicole is the focus of Francis's love throughout the novel, while Larry changes from being the object of Francis's hero worship and admiration to being an 'enemy' and the focus for his revenge.

The other, more minor, characters fall into distinct 'groups'.

Activity 1

a) Before reading on, decide how you might label the 'groups' of characters that make up the novel, besides the three main characters.

b) Consider the characters within these groups in relation to the two types of question that might be asked about them – either as 'groups' or as individuals.

- How does Cormier present them?
- How does Cormier use them?

The groups of characters include:

- Francis's family
- Francis's contemporaries at school and the Wreck Centre
- Religious figures – the nuns and a priest who have influenced Francis
- Francis's comrades in his platoon
- Other key characters from the war
- Veterans who 'hang out' at the St Jude Club
- Older members of the Frenchtown community
- Characters from the 'folklore' of Frenchtown – the incident at Grenier Hall

All the other characters in the novel are seen in relation to Francis, although it is clear that Nicole and Larry LaSalle, and Nicole and Marie LaCroix, also have relationships that exclude Francis. The veterans also have relationships with one another that were formed before Francis's arrival in Frenchtown.

In the exam, questions that focus on minor characters quite often ask about their function in relation to the themes of the novel.

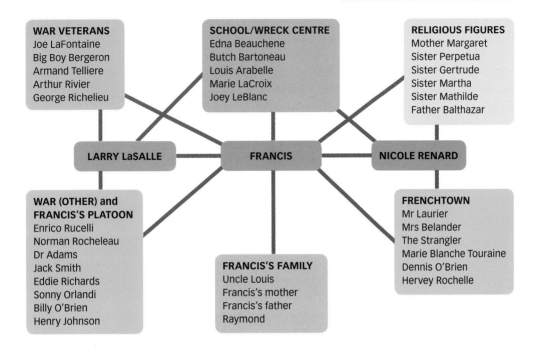

WAR VETERANS
Joe LaFontaine
Big Boy Bergeron
Armand Telliere
Arthur Rivier
George Richelieu

SCHOOL/WRECK CENTRE
Edna Beauchene
Butch Bartoneau
Louis Arabelle
Marie LaCroix
Joey LeBlanc

RELIGIOUS FIGURES
Mother Margaret
Sister Perpetua
Sister Gertrude
Sister Martha
Sister Mathilde
Father Balthazar

LARRY LaSALLE

FRANCIS

NICOLE RENARD

WAR (OTHER) and
FRANCIS'S PLATOON
Enrico Rucelli
Norman Rocheleau
Dr Adams
Jack Smith
Eddie Richards
Sonny Orlandi
Billy O'Brien
Henry Johnson

FRENCHTOWN
Mr Laurier
Mrs Belander
The Strangler
Marie Blanche Touraine
Dennis O'Brien
Hervey Rochelle

FRANCIS'S FAMILY
Uncle Louis
Francis's mother
Francis's father
Raymond

Main characters

Francis Joseph Cassavant

As the narrator, Francis appears in every chapter. It's important to remember that, because he is the narrator as well as the main character, Cormier presents Francis's character through both what he tells us directly and what he reports himself as saying and doing. In addition, all the other characters are presented as filtered through Francis's eyes.

However, Francis is not an **omniscient narrator** and this means that sometimes, as readers, we may suspect that Cormier is inviting us to question whether Francis's viewpoint is always strictly reliable. Francis can explain what he is thinking but cannot access the thoughts of the other characters. For example, we might wonder about Marie LaCroix's feelings for Francis in the early part of the novel. Cormier leaves it to the reader to suspect that, while Francis is fixated on Nicole, Marie may be feeling the same way about Francis, but Francis does not notice. Similarly, Francis does not really know what Nicole thinks about him at any point in the novel and there are occasions when the reader may feel that he interprets events incorrectly.

omniscient narrator a narrator who knows everything about the characters that he or she is writing about, including their inner thoughts and motivations, usually written in the third person

As a result, one aspect of Francis's character (his lack of awareness of other characters' feelings towards him) is revealed through this narrative technique, which allows the reader to see that there is a difference between the author's and the narrator's perspectives. This device does not apply to other characters in this novel.

Another aspect to consider, when writing about Francis's character, is that in many ways Nicole (as she says about herself in Chapter 16) is **'starting to find out what I am, who I really am…'** Francis could also be said to be in the process of discovering his true identity. Having taken pains to disguise himself from prying eyes in Frenchtown on his return from the war, it is interesting that he tells us that **'When I study myself in the mirror, I don't see me any more but a stranger slowly taking shape'** *(Chapter 10)*. Remember that Francis is only 18 years old at the beginning of the novel and that for much of the book he is only in his early teens; his true identity is still evolving.

If Francis was a real person, rather than a character in a novel, we might say he had had a difficult life.

- His mother died when he was six; his father died when he was 12.
- His girlfriend, whom he idolized, was raped in his hearing, by a man who they had both trusted and admired, and she blames Francis for not intervening.
- He contemplates suicide but enlists for the war instead and is exposed to terrible dangers and experiences, including losing comrades in combat, having to kill to survive and having his face blown off by a grenade.

Is it any surprise that Dr Adams's attempt in Chapter 1 to get Francis to develop a sense of humour has not had much success? However, we should not forget that Francis is not a real person. In the exam, you need to think about how Cormier *presents* or *uses* Francis, rather than thinking about his personality.

Identity and disguise are two themes that run through the novel

How Francis perceives himself versus how others perceive him

Through the use of the first-person narrative, Cormier is able to reveal that, for the majority of the novel, Francis appears to have a very low opinion of himself. In contrast, it is clear through what others say to Francis, and the way that they respond to him, that they consider him in a very positive light.

For example, look at the way in which Cormier uses Francis's very matter-of-fact way of describing his facial disfigurement to create a vivid yet negative picture of his looks. In Chapters 1 and 10, the language chosen to suggest that Francis has 'no face' is graphic and disturbing. However, the fact that he recounts his injuries with a complete lack of self-pity helps the reader to admire Francis, in spite of his self-proclaimed 'ugliness'.

Activity 2

Work in groups to pick out all the unpleasant words and phrases that Francis uses to describe his appearance, as well as the sound of his voice, in Chapters 1, 3 and 10.

What other characters say to Francis about himself is almost always positive.

Key quotations

"Poor boy." *(Mrs Belander, Chapters 1 and 3)*

"You deserve a good drink…" *(Arthur, Chapter 4)*

"You're a good boy, Francis." *(Uncle Louis, Chapter 5)*

"You deserve to be recognized, Francis… You're a goddam hero." *(Arthur, Chapter 6)*

"You have outstanding reflexes. You have a natural athletic gait." *(Larry, Chapter 7)*

"You're a natural." *(Larry, Chapter 7)*

"I love to watch you play…" *(Nicole, Chapter 7)*

"How about writing books? Didn't you win Sister Mathilde's medal for composition?" *(Nicole, Chapter 9)*

"Don't be afraid to show your face, Francis. That face, what's left of it, is a symbol of how brave you were…" *(Larry, Chapter 14)*

"You would have fallen on that grenade, anyway. All your instincts would have made you sacrifice yourself for your comrades." *(Larry, Chapter 14)*

"You have made us all proud." *(Sister Mathilde, Chapter 15)*

"You weren't to blame for what happened." *(Nicole, Chapter 16)*

"…you were part of the good times, Francis." *(Nicole, Chapter 16)*

"My good Francis. My table tennis champion. My Silver Star hero…" *(Nicole, Chapter 16).*

However, Francis tends to write about himself in a wholly negative way.

> **Key quotations**
>
> ...not deserving his [Arthur's] sympathy. *(Chapter 4)*
>
> Without talent for singing or dancing or arts and crafts... *(Chapter 5)*
>
> I'm rotten at everything... *(Chapter 7)*
>
> ...he was letting me win... *(Chapter 7)*
>
> I place my arm around his shoulder... a ridiculous gesture... *(Chapter 8)*
>
> "Oh, I could never write a book." *(Chapter 9)*
>
> A kind of bogeyman who does terrible things like letting his girl get hurt and attacked... *(Chapter 12)*
>
> ...as if it was part of the hell that I had earned... *(Chapter 12)*
>
> I had always wanted to be a hero, like Larry LaSalle and all the others, but had been a fake all along. *(Chapter 14)*
>
> "I was too much of a coward to kill myself." *(Chapter 14)*
>
> Still trying to make me better than I am. *(Chapter 14)*

On rare occasions he has confidence, inspired by the encouragement of Nicole and Larry LaSalle.

> **Key quotations**
>
> For the first time in my life, a tide of confidence swept through me. *(Chapter 7)*
>
> I knew no doubt... *(Chapter 7)*.

Contrasts with other characters

Another method that Cormier uses to present the character of Francis more clearly is to contrast him with other characters. For example, while Joey, Enrico and Larry are all very talkative, Francis is often silent or tongue-tied. Their confidence helps to emphasize Francis's diffidence – his shyness.

> **Activity 3**
>
> Work in groups to pick out all the references to Francis's shyness or feelings of awkwardness in Chapters 2, 3 and 5.

Francis's actions

Perhaps the most direct method that Cormier uses to present Francis is through what he does in the novel. This allows the reader to judge him by his actions.

If we look at the major events of the novel, we can identify the following as Francis's main actions (rather than what he feels).

- He wins a table tennis championship.
- He begins to date Nicole.
- He fails to intervene when he hears Larry LaSalle assaulting Nicole.
- He enlists in the army and kills two German soldiers in action.
- He throws himself on a grenade and is horribly disfigured.
- He returns to Frenchtown.
- He confronts Larry LaSalle.
- He tracks down Nicole.
- He boards a train.

For Francis, the most significant 'action' of all is his 'inaction' – his failure to take action when he realizes what Larry is doing to Nicole. It is this **sin of omission** that drives Francis to seek death in battle and then, having failed to die in combat, drives him in his mission to kill Larry.

We will see, when we look closely at themes on page 59, that Francis's sense of guilt is a crucial aspect of the novel; it defines him and it is only after he has been told, by both Larry and Nicole, that he was not to blame for what happened at the Wreck Centre that he can forgive himself and move on with his life. Cormier implies that he 'moves on' and becomes a writer; so writing the novel itself becomes his final action in the story.

> **sin of omission** in Catholic terminology, knowing the right thing to do, being capable of doing it and yet failing to do it

Francis's use of language

We have already seen that Francis, as narrator, uses a great deal of vocabulary linked to the Catholic Church, to the courtly love tradition and also to war and combat. He also writes in a fairly unemotional style and never over-dramatizes his story, except when recounting his vivid dream.

Activity 4

What differences can you detect between how Francis uses language as narrator and how he reports his own speech?

Nicole Renard

Nicole appears in Chapters 2, 5, 7, 9, 11, 12 and 16, but is also in Francis's thoughts in Chapters 1, 3, 4, 10, 14, 15 and 17.

Nicole is the most significant character in the novel, after Francis himself. She is the focus of Francis's emotional life in his early teen years; Larry LaSalle's assault on her is the motive for Francis's 'death-wish' and Francis's 'mission' in Frenchtown is intended to avenge the great wrong that Larry committed. If, at the end of the novel, Francis has any hopes for the future, they are to see if she **'could still be my girl'** *(Chapter 16)*. Nicole is Francis's alternative to **'the gun in my duffel bag'** *(Chapter 16)*. So how does Cormier present Nicole's character?

Cormier alerts the reader to Nicole's importance in the very first chapter, when, looking through the window of Mrs Belander's attic tenement, Francis glimpses both the steeple of St Jude's Church and **'the slanted roof of the Wreck Centre'** *(Chapter 1)* and he confides in us that **'I had not thought of her for, oh, maybe two hours'** *(Chapter 1)*. Later, as he kneels at the communion rail in St Jude's, Francis tells us that he prays for Nicole, adding a sense of mystery, by adding, **'wherever she may be'** *(Chapter 1)*.

> ### Activity 5
>
> Francis frequently refers to the 'absence' of Nicole in the novel. Go back through the text and make a note of each occasion when we hear Nicole's footsteps as she is leaving or where Francis tells us that she has 'gone'. (There are over 40 references.)

Francis describes Nicole as if she is a vision of perfection to him: **'Nicole Renard was small and slender, with shining black hair that fell to her shoulders. The pale purity of her face reminded me of the statue of St Thérèse in the niche next to Father Balthazar's confessional'** *(Chapter 2)*. The comparison to St Thérèse of Lisieux is significant, as there are parallels between Nicole and the late 19th-century saint. She became a nun in her early teens and was known as St Thérèse of the Holy Face. She believed that it was not necessary to accomplish heroic acts, but to live according to the 'little way', to show love for God. In her writings, she also began one prayer: "He sees the face disfigured, covered with blood! unrecognizable! [...] And yet the divine Child does not tremble."

St Thérèse became a nun when she was 15 years old

Initially, Nicole appears to be a symbol of saint-like purity. She is often wearing white – a white dress in Chapter 2 and a white blouse in Chapter 11. She is also associated with the nuns and spends time doing charitable work at the convent. As Francis gets older, he sees Nicole in a slightly different light; he no longer associates her with St Thérèse but **'the girls in certain magazines at Laurier's Drug Store who set my heart racing and my knees liquid'** *(Chapter 5)*.

Nicole transforms Francis from a tongue-tied and awkward boy who worshipped her from afar to a devoted boyfriend. He doesn't mind her playful teasing and he is even able to joke with her in return. However, Francis never treats her with anything less than respect and just before the incident at the Wreck Centre, his promise to buy Nicole a **'simple white gown'** *(Chapter 11)* that she admires, **'someday'** *(Chapter 11)*, suggests his romantic vision of a life spent together.

Both Francis and Nicole are essentially 'good' characters who have their innocence destroyed by Larry's calculated assault. Like Francis (and Enrico), Nicole speaks (in Chapter 16) of adjusting to her situation. When Larry raped Nicole, he not only robbed her of her virginity but also of her sense of security; his assault, like the **'sneak attack'** *(Chapter 8)* at Pearl Harbour, was so unexpected that its effects were devastating.

Francis's inability to act to save her also robbed her of any illusion that he could protect her. Despite having pledged his **'love and loyalty for ever'** *(Chapter 2)* like a knight, Francis did not rescue his 'damsel in distress' and this double disillusionment – betrayed by the two people she appeared to trust most – has transformed her physically as well as emotionally. (Francis does not immediately recognize Nicole when she enters the room in Chapter 16.)

Activity 6

Gather as many examples as you can of what Nicole says and what others say about her in the novel. Also make a list of her actions, to help you understand how Cormier presents Nicole.

Larry LaSalle

Larry appears in Chapters 5, 7, 9, 11 and 14, but he also features in Francis's thoughts or is discussed by others in Chapters 1, 3, 6, 10, 12, 13 and 16.

Larry is a much more complicated character than Nicole, who is wholly good. Larry is the **antagonist** of the novel, but, unlike a typical villain, he has elements of both good and evil in his character and could be considered an '**anti-hero**' figure.

> **antagonist** a character or group of characters whose function in a story is to oppose the main character (protagonist)
>
> **anti-hero** a main character who has significant bad qualities, but whom the reader finds it difficult to condemn because of their good or attractive ones

Let's consider Larry's attractive qualities first.

> **Key quotations**
>
> **A tall slim man stepped into view, a lock of blond hair tumbling over his forehead, a smile that revealed dazzling movie-star teeth.** *(Chapter 5)*
>
> **...the broad shoulders of an athlete and the narrow hips of a dancer. He was both.** *(Chapter 5)*
>
> **He swung the bat with authority...** *(Chapter 5)*
>
> **He was also a dancer, with a touch of Fred Astaire in his walk...** *(Chapter 5)*
>
> **But he was most of all a teacher, leading classes in dancing, arts and crafts, organizing a choral group, directing musical shows.** *(Chapter 5)*

His actions are equally impressive. In contrast to self-confessed 'talentless' Francis, Larry LaSalle's talents are many and various. In particular, just as he shows the young people how to transform '**lumps of clay into ashtrays**' *(Chapter 5)*, Larry is able to transform the young people themselves. He coaxes unlikely students into successful 'stars' including '**the notorious schoolyard bully, Butch Bartoneau**' who is coached patiently until his '**version of "The Dying Cowboy" brought tears to the eyes of everyone**' *(Chapter 5)* and '**tall and gawky and shy**' Edna Beauchene, who '**became the hit of the show**' *(Chapter 5)*.

Larry motivates and reassures all the kids: '**"You are all stars," Larry LaSalle always told us**' *(Chapter 5)*. In particular, his encouragement turns Francis from a depressed and bereaved young boy with low self-esteem into a table tennis champion and popular member of the Wreck Centre community.

Later, when Larry enlists, he appears as a perfect role model, not only courageous but modest. He does not allow the kids to cheer his decision but assures them, "**I'm just doing what millions of others are doing**" *(Chapter 9)*. As such, news of Larry's Silver Star for bravery in the '**jungles of Guadalcanal**' *(Chapter 11)* brings

The Guadalcanal landing was followed by six months of fighting Japanese troops

a rapturous response from the inhabitants of Frenchtown, who are proud to have a 'home-grown' hero. His capture of the machine gun nest, resulting in saving the lives of an entire platoon, becomes legendary in the town.

The reception at the city hall, when Larry returns on furlough, is another sign of the high esteem in which he is held and this esteem is never tarnished publicly. Newspaper clippings and photographs celebrating Larry's achievement as a war hero have pride of place in The Strangler's scrapbook, where a 'double page' is devoted to Larry and headed '**Lt. LaSalle Earns Silver Star**' *(Chapter 6)*. Only Nicole and Francis know that Larry had a darker side to his character.

Throughout the novel, Cormier refers to light and dark. These opposing images help to support the ambiguity of Larry's character. In Chapter 11, for example, there are a number of references to darkness, light and shadow – even the song *Dancing in the Dark* is significant.

Activity 7

1 See how many times photographs/pictures are referred to in the novel. Write a paragraph explaining why you think each of these is important.

2 **a)** There are a number of different songs referred to in the novel. Use the Internet to find the lyrics for the following songs:

- *Don't Sit Under the Apple Tree with Anyone Else but Me*
- *I'll Be with You in Apple-Blossom Time*
- *Dancing in the Dark*
- *Never in a Million Years Will There Be Another You*
- *There'll Be Bluebirds Over the White Cliffs of Dover.*

b) In pairs, write down as many ideas as you can for why you think the lyrics are important for this novel.

Although originally from Frenchtown, Larry's reappearance there as youth leader at the Wreck Centre also has some mystery attached to it and we are given early clues that he may have something to hide.

> **Key quotations**
>
> We knew little about him, however, and he discouraged questions. *(Chapter 5)*
>
> ...there were dark hints that he had "gotten into trouble" in New York City, a rumour Joey LeBlanc delighted in repeating, with raised eyebrows and a knowing look. *(Chapter 5)*

In Chapter 11, when he steps down from the train on the fateful day that will end in misery for Nicole and Francis, Larry is described as both a returning hero and as a dangerous aggressor.

> **Key quotations**
>
> ...resplendent in the green uniform with the lieutenant's bars on his shoulder and the ribbons and medals on his chest. He smiled, the old movie-star smile. *(Chapter 11)*
>
> His slenderness was knife-like now, lethal, his features sharper... I could picture him storming a hillside... bayonet fixed, grenades dangling from his belt, pumping bullets into the enemy... *(Chapter 11)*

These conflicting images of Larry help to define him as an anti-hero. Francis's impression of Larry as a fighting machine seems to anticipate the violent rape of Nicole.

One of the least attractive aspects of Larry LaSalle is his subtle manipulation of the young people at the Wreck Centre. Cormier chooses his vocabulary with care. Look at these examples.

> **Key quotations**
>
> Just as he had lured awkward girls into ballet classes... so did he bring a sudden importance to table tennis. He gave lessons tirelessly... encouraged girls to take up the sport. *(Chapter 7)*
>
> Larry LaSalle tossed her in the air... pressing her close, their faces almost touching, their lips only an inch or so from a kiss, before he allowed her to slip down against his body. *(Chapter 7)*
>
> He applauded her, his eyes looking deeply into hers, as she lay at his feet... *(Chapter 7)*
>
> ...he had been toying with me all along. *(Chapter 7)*

In Chapter 11, he surprises the young people with sweets and cola before manipulating a situation where he thinks he is alone with Nicole. The callousness of his actions is made more repellent by the fact that he appears to feel no shame, whistling as he leaves the scene of his crime.

In contrast, Larry's final appearance in Chapter 14 affects the reader differently. Cormier shows him as a broken man whose life has been wrecked by the war. Again, he selects vocabulary very carefully. He describes Larry's voice as **'a bit feeble'** *(Chapter 14)*. The fact that he is seated in a rocking chair suggests that the war has aged him prematurely and his looks are compared to a photograph, **'faded and yellowed with age'** *(Chapter 14)*. There is nothing here of the violent aggressor and, as he talks to Francis, completely unaware of the reason for his visit, he adopts his previous manner of support and concern. Larry tells Francis that he shouldn't be afraid to show his face as it represents his bravery. He tells him that he deserved to win the table tennis championship. Even after Francis has confronted him over Nicole and threatened to kill him, Larry continues to try to help Francis feel better about himself: **"All your instincts would have made you sacrifice yourself for your comrades"** *(Chapter 14)*.

However, he is still apparently without remorse for his assault on Nicole. He confides in Francis that he loves **'the sweet young things'** *(Chapter 14)*, shocking Francis into considering that perhaps Nicole was not the only victim of Larry's inappropriate attentions.

In Chapter 14, Cormier does not present Larry in a wholly negative light. Just as elsewhere in the novel, he presents the good and the bad together and the reader is left, as Francis is, pondering the question that Larry himself posed: **"Does that one sin of mine wipe away all the good things?"** *(Chapter 14)* There is even a hint that Cormier wants the reader to see something Christian in Larry's willingness to sacrifice his own life rather than allow Francis to commit murder.

Minor characters

In addition to the three main characters, Cormier has created many more characters who make up the community in Frenchtown or who add to Francis's experiences both at home in peace time and abroad during the war. Almost all of these characters are used by Cormier to help convey themes.

Francis's family

The family is referred to in Chapters 1, 2, 3, 5 and 12.

Although Francis's family are very minor characters in terms of the action of the novel, they are clearly important to Francis. With the exception of Uncle Louis, Francis's family have all died when the novel begins and the absence of family accounts for Francis's lack of confidence and also for his reliance on Larry and Nicole for emotional support: **'The loneliness of the tenement drove me to the Wreck Centre'** *(Chapter 5)*.

Francis's father had been a baseball star in younger days, a catcher whose nickname was Lefty and whose name Francis chooses not to disgrace by killing himself. Francis uses the name of his dead baby brother Raymond and his mother's maiden name Beaumont to create a false identity for himself at Mrs Belander's.

In the novel, Francis's family is used to convey the theme of heroism (baseball star) and to reinforce the importance of names.

Francis's friends at school and the Wreck Centre
Joey LeBlanc

Joey appears in Chapters 2, 5, 7 and 11.

- He is the closest thing to a best friend that Francis has at school; they go to the cinema together as youngsters.

- He is a confident boy who the nuns punish for often speaking 'out of turn' *(Chapter 5)*; his liveliness and cheeky banter contrasts with Francis's reserve and embarrassment.

- He annoys Francis by calling out to Nicole about her stockings in Chapter 2 and by (accurately) predicting that the Wreck Centre is still a place of 'doom' *(Chapter 5)*.

- He is more knowing than Francis and more suspicious of Larry: "Better watch out Mister LaSalle [...] Francis has got your number" *(Chapter 7)*.

- He dies in combat at Iwo Jima, shortly before the end of the war.

The Iwo Jima War Memorial at Arlington, Virginia honours all US marines who have died in defence of their country

Activity 8

Choose one of the minor characters from the novel. Write a diary entry from that character, explaining what they think of Francis, Nicole and Larry.

Marie LaCroix

Marie appears in Chapters 2, 11 and 16.

- She is Francis's neighbour and friends with both Nicole and Francis.
- Francis confesses his feelings for Nicole to Marie.
- Although Francis seems unaware of it, the reader suspects that Marie has feelings for him. She becomes less friendly with Nicole after Francis has confessed that he likes Nicole. She also writes to Nicole after she has left Frenchtown, sending news of Francis's Silver Star and of his injuries.
- Cormier uses Marie to show that, despite Francis's lack of confidence, she enjoys his company and this contributes to the reader's sympathetic response to Francis. Marie also adds humour (imitating Sister Mathilde's 'farts').

The following minor characters are members of the 'Wreck gang', so also subject to Larry's special attention, and contribute to the theme of 'transformation':

- **Louis Arabelle** – who Francis defeats in the table tennis championship
- **Butch Bartoneau** – the school bully who Larry teaches to sing
- **Edna Beauchene** – the shy, gawky girl who Larry teaches to dance.

Religious figures

The nuns and priest who have influenced Francis all add to the context of Catholicism in the novel, through references to prayers and their use of religious imagery and icons (statues, rosary beads, etc.). Cormier also uses some of them to emphasize the harsh discipline of the nuns who were Francis's teachers.

- **Sister Mathilde** – she awarded Francis a medal for composition and gives him Nicole's new address in Albany; she also tells Francis that he has "made us all proud" *(Chapter 3)*. Marie LaCroix jokes about her 'digestion' *(Chapter 2)*. Cormier uses her to move the plot forward (Nicole's address) and contribute to the themes of heroes and writing.
- **Sister Gertrude** – Francis follows her teaching 'from the mouth of Jesus' *(Chapter 1)* to 'pray for your enemies' *(Chapter 1)* when he prays for Larry LaSalle.
- **Sister Perpetua** – remembered by Francis and Norman Rocheleau in France for her use of the ruler 'for the slightest infraction' *(Chapter 3)*.
- **Sister Martha** – remembered by the veterans for "still knocking guys around in the eighth grade" *(Chapter 4)*.
- **Mother Margaret, the Mother Superior** – introduces Nicole to the seventh grade during Sister Mathilde's arithmetic class.

- **Father Balthazar** – the priest at St Jude's who offers up prayers **'from the pulpit for the safety of our men and women in the services'** *(Chapter 9)* and who is remembered for his long sermons by the veterans at the club; Francis was once one of his altar boys.

Francis's comrades in his platoon

They appear in Chapter 3 and are remembered in Chapter 17.

- **Eddie Richards** – whose fear is symbolized by his constant diarrhoea; he asks, **"What the hell are we doing here?"** *(Chapter 3)*.
- **Sonny Orlandi** – who mutters **'Jesus: meaning *I'm scared'*** *(Chapter 3)*.
- **Henry Johnson** – wounded in action, **'his chest ripped open by shrapnel'** *(Chapter 3)*.
- **Jack Smith** – died in action.
- **Billy O'Brien** – died in action.

Cormier uses these characters to underline the destructiveness of war and to add to the debate about what makes a hero. In Chapter 17, Francis decides that these ordinary soldiers were the real heroes of the war because they didn't run away.

Other key characters from the war
Enrico Rucelli

Enrico appears in Chapter 1 and is remembered in Chapters 4, 10 and 17. He is another badly wounded soldier who has lost his left arm and both legs; he is a friend to Francis and gave him his white silk scarf to cover his face. Francis confides in him about Nicole and Enrico is supportive. Like Joey, Enrico is a lively character, talkative and jokey, despite his suffering. Cormier uses him as a **foil** to Francis. Enrico contributes to the themes of physical destruction and disfigurement, as well as to the debate about what makes a hero.

> **foil** a character whose function in a story is to serve as a contrast to another character, in order to highlight one of their qualities

Dr Adams

Adams is referred to in Chapters 1, 10, 14, 15, 16 and 17. He is the cosmetic surgeon who offers Francis the hope of having his face repaired when the war is over. His sense of humour contrasts with Francis's terrible situation. Cormier uses him to suggest a possible future for Francis, which he attempts to destroy in Chapter 10 but appears to accept in Chapter 17. The 'future' is a theme in the novel.

Norman Rocheleau

Francis meets Norman (a fellow Frenchtown soldier) in the village in France where they drink red wine together like **'the heroes in a Hemingway novel'** *(Chapter 3)* and Norman tells Francis about Nicole's disappearance from Frenchtown. Cormier uses him to give information and to help convey the theme of heroes. He swaps his copy of *The Great Gatsby* (more heroes and anti-heroes) for Francis's cigarettes.

Veterans at the St Jude Club

The veterans appear in Chapters 4, 6 and 8.

- **Arthur Rivier** – the former baseball star whose experiences in the war have left him embittered, **'drunk and mournful [...] in the alley'** *(Chapter 17)*. He recognizes Francis's voice but respects his desire to remain anonymous; he admires him for his war heroism.
- **George Richelieu** – who lost his arm in the South Pacific.
- **Armand Telliere** – who suffers from flashbacks and hopes to become a policeman.
- **Joe LaFontaine** – he is going to become a teacher with the help of the GI Bill.
- **Big Boy Bergeron** – the war has wrecked his feet, but he hopes to become a fireman.

All the veterans help Cormier to present the theme of the destructiveness of war, as well as adding to the debate about heroes. George is disfigured, having lost an arm, but all are damaged in some way. Together they create a sense of camaraderie, which Francis says he would like to be a part of. He appears not to notice that, through their complete acceptance of him, he has become a part of this group (and thus they also contribute to depicting Francis's lack of self-worth). All consider their futures in a way that Francis will not allow himself to.

Adult members of the Frenchtown Community

- **Mrs Belander** – Francis's landlady in the 'present' and a kindly neighbour in his past, she appears in Chapters 1 and 3. She represents the sympathetic response of the citizens of Frenchtown to veterans.
- **The Strangler** – He appears in Chapter 6, tends the bar at the St Jude Club and keeps a scrapbook to commemorate the 'Frenchtown Warriors'. He calls Larry 'the best of the best' and drinks to his health. He represents the common opinion of Larry amongst the citizens of Frenchtown. Cormier also uses him as part of the series of 'champions' in the town. He was a wrestler who took on the travelling champions – a comment on the theme of 'heroes'.
- **Mr Laurier** – He appears in Chapter 9 and employed Francis in his store during the early part of the war. He reflects on the transformation from child to soldier **'fighting the Japs and the Germans'** *(Chapter 4)* in only five months. He clearly disapproves of putting inexperienced 'kids' into battle zones and comments on the theme of transformation.

Characters from the 'folklore' of Frenchtown

These characters are referred to in Chapter 5:

- **Marie Blanche Touraine** – the bride
- **Dennis O'Brien** – the groom
- **Hervey Rochelle** – the jilted fiancé who killed the bride, maimed the groom and then killed himself.

These characters foreshadow the love triangle and revenge action that is reflected in the plot involving Nicole, Larry and Francis. The destruction of the young lives of Nicole and Francis, which takes place at the Wreck Centre, mirrors the destruction of the bride and groom.

The importance of names in *Heroes*

One way an author can communicate information about a character is through their choice of names. Identity is a major theme in *Heroes* and therefore Cormier is very careful in selecting names for his characters. In many cases, the names appear to be significant.

It is possible that in naming Francis Joseph Cassavant, Cormier is alluding to one of the most famous names in Canada's musical history – Joseph Casavant. Joseph Casavant built organs for churches and cathedrals and, although it may be coincidental, this choice of name combines religious imagery with a sense of Francis as the 'organ' of the story. The name 'Francis', of course, links him firmly to the French–Canadians of Frenchtown.

Where relevant, show in your response to the exam question that you understand Cormier's intentions in giving his characters names that help him to convey key themes in the novel.

The name Nicole is of Greek origin and means 'people of victory'. It is possible that Cormier gave her this name to suggest that she, too, has heroic qualities for not allowing Larry's despicable actions to destroy her. Her ambitions to be a teacher suggest that she has survived.

Finally, Larry's surname LaSalle is also significant as he shares it with Saint Jean-Baptiste de La Salle, a priest in the 17th century who founded the 'Institute of the Brothers of the Christian Schools'. A model teacher himself, in the Catholic Church, de La Salle is also the patron saint of teachers. Cormier appears to have named Larry slightly **ironically** as he betrays the trust of those he is supposed to be leading.

irony the discrepancy between what a character could be expected to do and what they actually do, often for comic effect

Writing about characters

Upgrade

An understanding of the characters of *Heroes* is essential as you may be asked to write about one or more characters in your exam. Equally important is understanding how the author presents the character and how the author uses the character to communicate their ideas with the reader.

It is also worth considering how the author uses language to present the characters, in particular noting the ways in which Cormier engages and influences the reader through the use of the first-person perspective.

When you are considering the methods that Cormier uses to present character, you may like to consider:

- what the character looks like/sounds like
- what they say – about themselves and about others
- what others say about the character
- contrast/comparison with other characters
- what the character does – their actions and/or reactions in the novel
- the kind of language the character uses when speaking
- the character's name.

When thinking about how he uses his characters, think about whether they:

- give information
- develop the plot
- comment on or represent specific themes
- act as a foil or contrast to other characters
- alter the mood or atmosphere or bring about a change in the story
- act as a mouthpiece for the author's view.

Narrative technique

Cormier's approach to the story of Francis Cassavant is very much in keeping with the genre known as a **'coming of age'** narrative, for which the official literary term is a **'Bildungsroman'**.

Through his first-person narrative, written as if by an ordinary 18-year-old, Cormier depicts Francis's transformation from a shy young boy who initially sees the fight against the 'Japs' and the Germans as a heroic 'crusade', to a damaged individual who sees no future for himself beyond his 'mission'. Once Francis has achieved his 'mission' and has been relieved of his guilt by both Larry LaSalle and Nicole, he is finally able to complete his process of 'growing up' and move on to his future, accepting the world for what it is rather than for what he would like it to be.

Cormier makes the reader care for Francis through his unsentimental tone, his apparent lack of self-pity and by making it seem as if Francis is speaking to the reader directly. The use of short paragraphs also helps him to create the impression of speech.

On a number of occasions, Francis comments directly on the action that he is reporting. For example:

Key quotations

Don't take him wrong, please. *(Chapter 1)*

Was the look that passed between us that first day a wish or my imagination? *(Chapter 2)*

And I had not yet killed anybody. *(Chapter 3)*

It scares me, how easy it is to lie. *(Chapter 3)*

Bildungsroman a literary genre focused on the main character's psychological and moral growth

coming of age growing into adulthood through knowledge and experience

---

On other occasions, he uses italics to highlight what he was thinking during the conversation that he is reporting. For example, in Chapter 16 during his reunion with Nicole, she says, **"I'm fine"**, but the narrator adds *'You don't sound fine'* – a line that is not spoken to Nicole.

Later in the same chapter when Nicole asks **"To see if I had survived?"** *(Chapter 16)* the narrator adds, *'To see if maybe you could still be my girl. Which could maybe change my mind about the gun in my duffel bag'* *(Chapter 16)*. Again, Francis does not say this out loud. These techniques make the reader sympathize with the narrator, Francis.

Language devices

There are a number of striking features about Robert Cormier's use of language in *Heroes*.

Simple sentence construction and uncomplicated words

Throughout the novel, Cormier uses short sentences and simple vocabulary. This links to Francis's first-person narrative, imitating speech patterns and allowing the reader to feel he is speaking directly to us.

> **Key quotations**
>
> Later, I light a candle in St Jude's Church. *(Chapter 1)*
>
> I turned to find her there. *(Chapter 7)*
>
> We always did what Larry told us to do. *(Chapter 11)*
>
> I take the gun out of my pocket. *(Chapter 14)*
>
> I should do all those things. *(Chapter 17)*

In the Catholic Church, lighting a candle indicates saying a prayer for someone and can also symbolize hope

Activity 1

As well as using short sentences, Cormier also uses many very short 'paragraphs' in this novel. Re-read the first few pages of Chapter 1, up to the line 'my mission was about to begin', and see how many paragraphs you can find that are less than a line in length. What is the effect of structuring Francis's ideas into very short 'bites'? How does it affect your reading of the novel?

Vocabulary related to religion, courtly love or war

Religion, courtly love and war are key themes in *Heroes* and Cormier emphasizes this by using vocabulary related to all three throughout the novel. Here are some examples.

Key quotations

Religion

I was impatient to reach the age when I could join them in that great crusade for freedom. *(Chapter 4)*

"I'm rotten at everything," I confessed. *(Chapter 7)*

The smell of ashes fills the air, a damp incense burning for Larry LaSalle's home-coming. *(Chapter 10)*

Courtly love

My name had been on her lips! *(Chapter 2)*

I wondered if he suspected my secret love for her. *(Chapter 7)*

"I'll never leave you." *(Chapter 11)*

War

I feel like a spy in disguise… *(Chapter 3)*

He could tap-dance with machine-gun speed… *(Chapter 5)*

How many young girls had been invaded by him? *(Chapter 14)*

Figurative language

Cormier uses **figurative language** – **metaphors** and **similes** – in order to help his readers imagine what he is describing as clearly as possible.

atmosphere the mood created by a piece of writing

figurative language the collective name for simile, metaphor and personification; language which is not to be taken literally

metaphor a comparison of one thing to another to make a description more vivid; a metaphor states that one thing is the other

motif a repeated idea, phrase or word that the reader notices again and again in a text, and which supports the themes in a text

simile a comparison of one thing to another to make a description more vivid, using the words 'like' or 'as' to make the comparison

---

Key quotations

Similes

German soldiers in white uniforms appear like grim ghosts... *(Chapter 3)*

...a whimpering, like a small animal caught and trapped... *(Chapter 11)*

the sound like cloth ripping *(Chapter 12)*

Metaphors

I break the mood with the question that has been burning inside me *(Chapter 6)*

...her face caught in the slash of moonlight... *(Chapter 11)*

marvelling again how Larry LaSalle was always one step ahead of us *(Chapter 14)*

Repetition

Another technique used by Cormier to highlight key themes and **motifs** is repetition of particular words. For example:

- 'hero' or 'heroes' is repeated over 20 times
- 'steps' or 'foot-steps' appears over 40 times
- 'star', 'movie-star' or 'Silver Star' appears over 20 times
- 'champion', 'champ' or 'championship' is repeated over 10 times
- 'name' appears over 12 times and 'identity', 'disguise' or 'anonymity' appear over 20 times
- 'recognition' appears over 10 times.

References to the five senses

Cormier uses references to the five senses throughout *Heroes*, adding to the **atmosphere** and creating a vivid impression of Francis's experiences.

...get yourself to a home for the <u>blind</u>... **(sight)** *(Chapter 1)*

...making a <u>sound</u> like a saw going through wood... **(hearing)** *(Chapter 1)*

...you could see the <u>pain</u> flashing in his eyes... **(touch)** *(Chapter 1)*

...the <u>fragrance</u> of old incense... **(smell)** *(Chapter 1)*

I lost my <u>appetite</u> somewhere in France... **(taste)** *(Chapter 3)*

References to body parts

Cormier makes frequent references to body parts, particularly to parts of the face, reminding the reader of what Francis has lost through his actions.

In the images of Nicole that Francis carries with him, she is often dancing or wearing white

> **Key quotations**
>
> "You've got a big <u>mouth</u>" *(Chapter 2)*
>
> ...releasing the smoke through his <u>mouth and nostrils</u>... *(Chapter 3)*
>
> ...curiosity remaining in his <u>eyes</u>... *(Chapter 3)*
>
> ...catching flashes of her white <u>thighs</u>... *(Chapter 5)*
>
> ...his <u>arm</u> is buried somewhere in the South Pacific... *(Chapter 6)*
>
> ...our <u>lips</u> briefly touching... *(Chapter 9)*
>
> ...his features sharper, <u>nose and cheek-bones</u>... *(Chapter 11)*
>
> ...her warm <u>cheek</u> rested against mine... *(Chapter 11)*

> **Activity 2**
>
> Discuss, using specific examples, what you feel is significant about the language that Cormier uses in *Heroes*. What is the effect or impact of the examples you have chosen?

References to opposites

References are made throughout the novel to opposites such as light and dark, heat and cold, etc. These act as motifs throughout the novel, often helping to mirror Francis's moods.

> **Key quotations**
>
> ...the sweat <u>warm</u> on my flesh, but in a minute the sweat turns <u>icy</u>... *(Chapter 3)*
>
> Numbed, I stepped out of the <u>moonlight's</u> rays, wanting to hide in the <u>dark</u>. *(Chapter 11)*
>
> The <u>coldness</u> of the hallway hits the <u>warmth</u> of my flesh and I shiver. *(Chapter 14)*
>
> ...the <u>smile</u> turns into a <u>grimace</u> and I wonder what he's thinking of... *(Chapter 17)*

These are only a few examples of some of the key aspects of Cormier's writing in *Heroes*. Remember that, in addition to these, Cormier uses the basic tool that all writers employ to engage the reader – a varied vocabulary, including the literary devices on the following page.

Feature	Examples
Adjectives	such sweet voices in the air (Chapter 4)
	"I think I have the perfect sport for you" (Chapter 7)
Adverbs	whistling softly as he stepped through the doorway (Chapter 11)
	'smiling dreamily' (Chapter 17)
Alliteration	Familiar faces turn towards me. (Chapter 4)
	my moment of triumph tarnished and trashed (Chapter 7)
Colloquial language	"You've got a big mouth," I told Joey (Chapter 2)
	"Better watch out, Mr LaSalle… Francis has got your number." (Chapter 7)
Imagery	bird-like and graceful as she danced (Chapter 5)
	a woman in a simple white gown that clung to her body like whipped cream (Chapter 11)
	His slenderness was knife-like now (Chapter 11)
Onomatopoeia	I explode into wakefulness along with the booming artillery (Chapter 3)
	The scratching of the needle stopped. (Chapter 11)
Personification	A heat wave gripped Frenchtown (Chapter 12)
	A deep sadness settles on me as if winter had invaded my bones. (Chapter 14)
Synaesthesia	my flesh burned with the echo of her touch (Chapter 7)

alliteration the repetition of the same letter or sound at the beginning of words close to one another

colloquial language informal, everyday speech

onomatopoeia the use of words which sound like the thing or process they describe

personification a type of metaphor where human qualities are given to objects or ideas

synaesthesia a literary device where words associated with one sense are used to describe another sense

Writing about language

Upgrade

An understanding of the language of *Heroes* is essential. You might consider:

- The ways in which language is used to create characters and highlight key themes.

- The impact created for the reader through Cormier's choice of vocabulary and use of literary techniques.

- The writer's use of language to help present characters, in particular, noting the ways in which Cormier engages and influences the reader through the use of the first-person perspective.

Major themes

If you have been reading through this guide chapter by chapter, by now you will have had plenty of opportunity to think about the various themes that Cormier deals with in *Heroes*. One of the interesting things about the way Cormier has shaped the novel is his use of **antithetical** (opposite) ideas – 'paired' themes.

Heroism and cowardice

> **Key quotations**
>
> **"If I want one thing, it would be to have you look at me again the way you did at the Wreck Centre. When I was the big hero you say I was."**
> *(Larry, Chapter 14)*

Heroism is the most important theme in the novel. Cormier called the novel *Heroes* and the concept of heroism has a place in every chapter, even if it is only a passing reference. Cormier uses all the methods at his disposal to convey the importance of the theme of heroism in this novel and to explore what it really means to be a hero.

Methods	Theme: Heroism
Title of the novel	*Heroes*
Content of the novel	The novel is largely about what it means to be a hero.
Characters discuss the theme	There are three main conversations about heroism to be found in Chapters 6, 14 and 16; additionally, Francis reflects on the theme in Chapter 17.
Characters, through their actions, 'do' the theme	Larry LaSalle and Francis both earn the Silver Star military medal for heroism and Francis concludes, at the end of the novel, that the rest of his platoon were the **'real heroes'** *(Chapter 17)*.
The theme is referred to in repeated motifs and/ or figurative language	The word 'heroes' is used frequently and echoed in numerous references to stars, champions, medals and trophies.

Methods	Theme: Heroism
The author/narrator refers directly to the theme	Throughout the novel Francis denies that he is a hero in conversations with others and in **asides** to the reader. **I am not a hero, of course.** *(Chapter 1)* **I am not the hero he thinks I am, not like the other veterans.** *(Chapter 4)* **I had never been a hero in such places...** *(Chapter 5)* **Noble deaths. The deaths of heroes. How could I die by leaping from a steeple?** *(Chapter 12)* **"I am not a hero," I tell him.** *(Chapter 14)* **Hero. The word hangs in the air.** *(Chapter 16)*

antithesis contrasting ideas or words that are balanced against one another

aside a speech in a play given by an actor directly to the audience, unheard by the other characters (in this context, Francis's unspoken thoughts)

The USA honour their war dead as heroes in the American War Cemetery at Omaha Beach in Normandy, France

In *Heroes*, the theme of heroism is also paired with its related or antithetical theme – cowardice. Francis contrasts being a hero with being a coward on several occasions, for example, in Chapters 3, 14 and 16. He also contrasts heroism with being a 'fake', as he terms himself, despite everyone else (Arthur Rivier, Nicole, Larry, Sister Mathilde) apparently seeing him as a 'hero'. None of his actions appear 'cowardly' to the reader – only to himself.

Remember that the different perspectives on Francis's heroic or cowardly qualities are created through Cormier's narrative technique (i.e. the narrator does not always see things as they really are). It is important to mention this in your exam response when discussing Francis's heroism or cowardice.

Larry LaSalle is also celebrated by all the citizens of Frenchtown as a Silver Star hero due to his heroic acts in wartime. Yet his manipulation of Francis and his despicable assault on Nicole are the acts of a coward, since he dare not do anything until he believes Francis (Nicole's protector) has gone home.

Towards the end of the novel, Francis comes to see his fellow soldiers as 'heroes' despite the fact that they were 'scared'. He realizes that he and the other young men were **'scared kids not born to fight and kill. Who were not only there but who stayed, did not run away'** *(Chapter 17)*. He concludes that this is real heroism.

Activity 1

1. Take time to think about whether anybody can actually be a 'hero' unless somebody else sees them as one. Do you think anyone actually sees themselves as a 'hero'? Isn't 'hero' a label we give to people who do things that we believe to be beyond our own abilities or daring? Is Francis right to conclude that it is the most ordinary people, put into extraordinary situations, who become heroes in the eyes of those who were not there? Arrange yourselves into small groups to discuss these questions.

2. In pairs, make a list of all the characters in the novel who might be considered to be 'heroes', 'stars' or 'champions'.

Identity and anonymity

In the novel, the theme of identity and anonymity is also linked with recognition, names and disguise, and relates to each of the main characters.

Francis arrives in Frenchtown determined to conceal his identity in order to carry out his 'mission'; Arthur respects his wish for anonymity at the St Jude Club. The destruction of his face has gone a long way towards protecting his anonymity. Earlier, Francis had also chosen to enlist rather than commit suicide, in order to protect his family name from being damaged.

Larry's true identity is always hidden. There are rumours of his life before arriving in Frenchtown (Joey asks: **"Is that his real name?"** *(Chapter 5)*), but his true 'identity' as a callous destroyer of innocence is concealed beneath the 'mask' of leader/teacher/hero. The community generally accepts this false identity and his appearances on the newsreels and in newspapers supports the idealized view of who he is – **'it was our Larry LaSalle, all right'** *(Chapter 9)*.

Nicole's name runs through Francis's thoughts throughout the novel. He likens her both to a saint and to a pin-up girl but when he visits her in Chapter 16, he says that her appearance has changed almost beyond recognition. At this point she states that she is finding out who she really is.

There are other references to identity and to disguise in the novel, such as when the mysterious baseball player comes to Frenchtown and people suspect him of being **'a major league player in disguise'** *(Chapter 6)*. Many characters hide their true feelings and struggles behind a 'mask'. The theme also ties in to the contrast, as Cormier presents it, between the war as those at home see it and as it actually is.

Love and war

The paired themes of love and war dominate the action of the novel and Francis's love for Nicole is played out against the backdrop of war. The descriptions of Francis's own experience of warfare and the experiences of his fellow veterans are used to reveal the senseless waste of youth that occurs in war.

Guilt and forgiveness

As noted before, there are many references in *Heroes* to guilt and forgiveness, and many of these are linked to the Catholic concepts of sin and redemption.

The key event in question is, of course, Larry's assault on Nicole and Francis failing to intervene. After the incident, when Francis realizes that Nicole blames him for not saving her, he is consumed with a sense of guilt so extreme that it makes him suicidal (even though this is itself considered one of the gravest sins). It is this guilt that leads him to enlist and to throw himself on a grenade. But despite his disfigurement and the lives he saves, Francis's sense of guilt is not lessened. In fact, it is intensified by others' perception of him as a hero.

In contrast, Larry appears to feel little guilt for what he did to Nicole, although his shock at Francis's hatred for him seems to affect him more. He asks Francis one of the most important questions of the novel: **"Does that one sin of mine wipe away all the good things?"** *(Chapter 14)* Larry tries to relieve Francis's sense of guilt, telling him he was not to blame for what happened at the Wreck Centre. In the end, he chooses to take his own life to prevent Francis from committing the sin/crime of murder. He tells Francis: **"Leave everything here, the war, what happened at the Wreck Centre, leave it all behind, with me"** *(Chapter 14)*.

Nicole, too, seems to feel guilt for having blamed Francis, apologizing to him in Chapter 16 and immediately offering him forgiveness (although it is clear she cannot forget what has happened). Francis does not respond directly but he does appear to be able to move forward, having seen both Larry and Nicole for the last time and heard that they do not blame him. It is up to the reader to decide whether Francis has found the redemption and forgiveness he was searching for.

Activity 2

See if you can answer Larry's question. Does his sin wipe away the good things he has done? In pairs, make a list of Larry's good actions and then of his bad actions. Which is the longer list? Does Larry do more harm than good?

Truth and lies

This is another theme that is largely connected to Francis and to his perception of himself, as well as to the themes of identity and anonymity. He regularly describes things that he says – especially when he is talking about the future – as 'lies' and we know that he has practised deceit by forging his date of birth in order to be accepted into the forces. Here are other examples of the lies Francis tells:

- He lies to Mrs Belander about his family, **'Here is the point where my life becomes a lie'** *(Chapter 3)*.

- He tells Sister Mathilde that a doctor **"is going to help me"** *(Chapter 15)* but then comments to the reader: **'I wonder if it's a special sin to lie to a nun'** *(Chapter 15)*.

- Similarly, when he tells Nicole of his intention to **"Go to high school. College later"** *(Chapter 16)* he adds, as if talking directly to the reader, **'The words sound flat and false to my ears'** *(Chapter 16)*.

Good and evil

In common with many novels, plays and films, *Heroes* presents the struggle between good and evil. Sometimes this is a struggle between two opposing 'sides', for example, in the war, where the Americans saw themselves as the force of 'good' fighting the 'evil' of **'the Japs and the Germans'** *(Chapter 3)*. The fact that Francis describes this as a **'crusade'** *(Chapter 4)* emphasizes this. Sometimes, the struggle is between two individuals, as occurs when Francis confronts Larry about his attack on Nicole. However, at other times, the struggle is internal. In Chapter 12, Francis struggles with his conscience and ends up deciding not to kill himself, while in Chapter 14, Larry's inner struggle between good and evil ends with him taking his own life.

The unprovoked Japanese attack on Pearl Harbour in 1941 brought the USA into the Second World War

Books, reading and writing

While the major themes of heroism and identity, guilt and forgiveness, and good and evil are quite easy to spot as you read the novel, you may not have noticed the significance of one of Cormier's other concerns – books, reading and writing.

Francis's journey from childhood to adulthood also sees him growing from a studious type of child whose ambition is to **"read every book in the Monument Public Library"** *(Chapter 9)* to a man who appears to be about to write his first book – about the **'real heroes'** *(Chapter 17)*.

Cormier includes numerous references to literature throughout the novel. Sometimes Francis tells us what he is reading or what books he and Nicole admire, for example, *A Farewell to Arms* or *Rebecca* in Chapter 9. Sometimes there are brief references to characters from literature, which Cormier uses to help us picture some of the characters in *Heroes*. For example, in Chapter 1, Francis compares himself to the Hunchback of Notre Dame: **'my face like a gargoyle and the duffel bag like a lump on my back'**. In Chapter 11, Larry is compared to **'a bright Pied Piper'** who had helped the children **'in the bleakness of the Depression'**.

It's important to recognize that all the literary references have greater significance than appears on the surface, as each one relates directly either to the plot of *Heroes* or to its themes.

Text	Plot/Characters	Relevance to *Heroes*
The Hunchback of Notre Dame by Victor Hugo	Quasimodo, a deformed hunchback, falls in love with Esmeralda, a gypsy woman who is condemned to death for being suspected as a witch. Quasimodo swings down from the bell tower of Notre Dame Cathedral and saves her life.	In Chapter 1, Francis compares himself to Quasimodo. However, he was unable to save his love from harm.
The Sun Also Rises by Ernest Hemingway	Jake Barnes, a journalist, returns from the war with a wound that has left him impotent. He is involved in a love triangle with Lady Brett Ashley. The novel deals with the consequences of war and unrequited love.	Francis is reading this novel in Chapter 2. It is clearly relevant to him and his fellow veterans who are damaged in the war. The 'triangular' love story echoes the Francis/Nicole/Larry plot. Hemingway's sparse writing style is echoed in *Heroes*. Remember that reading this novel makes Francis **'wonder if anyone, including me, could become a writer'** *(Chapter 2)*.

Text	Plot/Characters	Relevance to *Heroes*
The Great Gatsby by F. Scott Fitzgerald	Nick Carraway, a returning soldier from the First World War, narrates the story of Gatsby, who is in love with Daisy Buchanan. Daisy's husband, Tom, is having an affair with Myrtle Wilson who Daisy kills, accidentally, while driving Gatsby's car. Gatsby takes the blame for Myrtle's death and is then shot dead by her jealous husband, George. George Wilson then shoots himself.	Francis swaps his cigarette ration for this book when he meets Norman Rochelle in Chapter 3. The revenge action and complex web of relationships echo the shooting in Grenier Hall, as well as Francis's own revenge mission. Murder and suicide feature as themes in both *The Great Gatsby* and *Heroes*.
A Farewell to Arms by Ernest Hemingway	Written from the perspective of Frederick Henry, this first-person narrative relates the doomed love affair between Henry and a British nurse, Catherine Barkley. Hemingway presents a personal tragedy against the background of the wider destruction caused by the First World War.	Francis describes this as his favourite book in Chapter 9; Nicole says she wept at the end of the novel. The failed love affair and the background of war are clearly linked to Francis and Nicole.
Rebecca by Daphne Du Maurier	This very complicated story is written as if by Rebecca, the new bride of Maxim De Winter, a widower whose young and beautiful first wife appears to have drowned in mysterious circumstances. Finally it is revealed that Maxim killed his wife when she taunted him about her many affairs. We then discover she had just been diagnosed with an inoperable cancer and had intentionally provoked Maxim to shoot her as she could neither face the pain and suffering of the cancer, nor bear to take her own life.	Larry LaSalle's suicide has some echoes of the need to avoid suffering and Francis's threat to shoot him parallels Maxim's anger at his wife's infidelity. Unlike Mrs de Winter, however, Larry does not allow Francis to commit the sin and crime of murder to end his misery, but shoots himself as an act of atonement. Complicated love triangles are a feature of both books.
The Pied Piper of Hamelin	In this folktale (turned into a famous poem by Robert Browning) the Pied Piper is seen as a saviour for ridding Hamelin of a plague of rats, but when the townsfolk fail to pay him for his services, he lures all the children to their deaths.	There are echoes here of Larry luring the children of the Wreck Centre into destruction.

The fable turns sinister when the Pied Piper lures away the children of Hamelin

If you are answering a question that includes reference to one of these novels/ tales, make sure you explain its relevance to the plot and characters of *Heroes*.

Activity 3

In small groups, work through the list of themes mentioned in this chapter and make a theme table for each of them, using the table for heroism on pages 56–57 as your template.

Minor themes

Of course, in this richly complex novel, there are many other themes, including:

- **Transformation**
  Initially, Larry helps to transform young people in a positive way. However, both Nicole and Francis are transformed in a negative way by Larry's actions.

- **Destruction/Damage/Disfigurement/Wreck**
  The Wreck Centre is seen as a place of 'doom' and what happens there wrecks the lives of Nicole, Francis and, ultimately, Larry. Cormier uses the Wreck Centre as a symbol of 'damage' and 'doom'. The war is also a source of much suffering and damage to all the characters that Cormier describes, especially to Francis's platoon and to the veterans at the St Jude Club.

- **Revenge**
  Francis's attempt to take revenge on Larry is anticipated by the story of Grenier Hall and the killing of the bride, as well as being echoed in the references to some of the books – *The Great Gatsby*, for example.
- **Champions/Knights/Stars/Medals/Prizes/Trophies**
- **Loss and absence/Loneliness**

Additionally, there are repeated motifs:

- **The five senses** are very important in this novel as we noted on pages 51–52. Below are just a few examples of the many things Francis tells us that he hears:

Key quotations

...making a sound like a saw going through wood... *(Chapter 1)*

quiet curses floating on the air, grunts and hisses and farts *(Chapter 3)*

...the juke-box plays *I'll Be with You in Apple Blossom Time*, such sweet voices in the air. *(Chapter 4)*

I swung the paddle, struck the ball with a satisfying plop... *(Chapter 7)*

The sound of a pistol shot cracks the air. [...] The sound from this distance is almost like a ping-pong ball striking the table. *(Chapter 14)*

The sound of the doorbell echoes unendingly through the long corridors. *(Chapter 15)*

The ball when it lands doesn't have the sharp sound of a ping-pong ball on a table... *(Chapter 16)*

- **Light/dark** – sensations (associated with sight)
- **Heat/cold** – sensations (associated with touch)
- **Pain and suffering** – sensations (associated with touch)
- **Footsteps** – sensations (associated with hearing); charting the journeys of Francis, Nicole and Larry throughout the novel.

All of these themes and motifs help Cormier to enrich the simple story that lies at the heart of the novel – Francis's journey from childhood to adulthood and his growing understanding of the world.

Activity 4

Use each of the bullet points above as a heading for your notes. Which characters are most clearly linked to each theme?

Writing about themes

Upgrade

In your exam, you may be asked to write about an individual theme or a pair of themes. You are likely to be asked how the author presents the theme and/or what is the importance of the theme. Other points you could consider are:

- The ways in which different characters are related to the novel's themes.

- The methods Cormier uses to highlight key themes, including how he uses literary techniques to support and highlight themes.

Exam skills

There are several practical steps you can take to make sure that you are fully prepared for the challenges of the exam.

Step 1: Make sure you know *Heroes* really well

It's a short novel. Try to read it at least three times before you go into the exam. Each time you re-read it, stop after each chapter and jot down some notes under the headings we have used in this book; pick out things that strike you about:

- plot and structure
- context
- characters
- language
- themes.

Just before the exam, re-read Chapter 1 of this book (Plot and Structure).

Step 2: Revision

Go back through this book and check that you have completed all of the activities, either in class, in pairs or groups, or on your own. Re-read all the Upgrade sections in this book, where you will find tips for tackling questions and for improving your answers. Re-read all the key quotations from *Heroes* that appear in this book. Try to memorize as many as you can.

Plan potential questions. Open the novel randomly at any chapter, choose a single page and try to write at least one paragraph about the significance of that section in relation to:

- plot and structure
- context
- characters
- language
- themes.

Choose one of the following themes from the novel and practise writing a page or more about its importance in the novel:

- books, reading and writing
- guilt and forgiveness
- recognition and anonymity
- revenge
- wreck and destruction.

Choose one of the following characters from the novel and practise writing a page or more about their importance in the novel:

- Marie LaCroix
- Sister Mathilde
- Joey LeBlanc
- Arthur Rivier.

You must be prepared to write about Francis, Nicole and Larry LaSalle. Use the guidance in Chapter 3 of this book (Characters) to help you to write a detailed plan for the following questions:

- Do you consider Larry LaSalle to be a hero, a villain or both in *Heroes*?
- How does the author use the character of Nicole in *Heroes*?
- How does Cormier present the character of Francis Cassavant in *Heroes*?

Activity 1

In pairs, swap your pages and see what you and your partner have written. Try to improve your partner's work and vice versa.

Step 3: Improving exam technique

Brushing up on exam technique is really worth the effort and can make a real difference to your overall grade. Understanding 'examiner-speak' is a vital skill to acquire. We have already considered different types of question about character and themes in Chapters 3 and 5. Remind yourselves of these before looking at the further examples below.

Essay-style questions

Most essay-style questions (those that are not based on a printed extract) will ask you to write about plot (the events that take place in the novel), character or themes. However, these questions will never require a simple description of these elements. You will always be expected to consider either the ways in which these aspects are presented or their significance in the novel.

Here are some typical essay-style questions, with the 'examiner-speak' words and phrases in bold. This is followed by an explanation of what each question requires and an outline plan for tackling the question.

Explore the importance of events at the Wreck Centre to the novel.

This question is about the **plot/action** of the novel. 'Explore' means 'look at the events from a number of different angles'. A good way to tackle questions like these is to consider the importance of the events in relation to plot and structure, context, characters and themes.

So, for this specific question, you might make the following plan.

Plot – the Wreck Centre is central to the plot; it's the place where the key events of the novel occur:

- the grooming of the young people by Larry
- Francis's success in the championship
- the developing friendship between Francis and Nicole
- the rape of Nicole
- the earlier tragic events at Grenier Hall anticipate the 'doom' of the Wreck Centre.

Context – the Wreck Centre is central to the youth culture in the novel, offering the kids some purpose as well as recreation.

Characters – events here are crucial to showing character:

- Larry's good and bad qualities are highlighted at the Wreck Centre
- it is the scene of Francis's greatest triumph (table tennis) and shame (not acting to save Nicole)
- Nicole loses her innocence here
- all three characters are changed forever.

Themes – the Wreck Centre is a symbol for some of the main themes:

- wreck and destruction are key themes in the novel
- Larry becomes a hero for the Wreck Centre gang
- Cormier makes a comparison between Larry and the Pied Piper of Hamelin in his role at the Wreck Centre.

> **How does Cormier create** sympathy for Francis when he returns from the war?

This question is about **character** and the 'how' part of the question refers to the **writer's methods**. You will remember, from Chapter 3, that the writer's methods for creating character include:

- what the character looks like/sounds like
- what the character says about himself/herself and about others
- what others say about the character
- contrast/comparison with other characters

- what the character does: his/her actions and/or reactions in the novel
- the kind of language the character uses when speaking
- the character's name.

Additionally, where the question is about Francis, you will need to mention the narrative voice.

In this specific question, make sure that all the points you make are related to creating **sympathy** for Francis through these methods. Use the list above as headings for your plan and make sure you refer to each aspect in your answer.

Remind yourself of the demands for the 'character' questions that require you to consider a character's importance or function in the novel. (See page 47.)

> **How does the writer present** the theme of war in the novel?

This question is about **theme**, with the 'how does the writer present' part of the question referring to the **writer's methods**. You will remember from Chapter 5 that the writer's methods for presenting themes include:

- the title of the novel
- the content of the novel
- whether characters discuss the theme
- whether characters, through their actions, 'do' the theme
- whether the theme is referred to in repeated motifs and/or in figurative language
- whether the theme is presented as a contrast or opposite to another theme
- whether the author/narrator refers directly to the theme.

Use the list above as headings for your plan and make sure you refer to each relevant aspect in your answer.

Remind yourself of the demands for the 'theme' questions that require you to consider a theme's importance in the novel. (See page 65.)

Extract-based questions

For extract-based questions you should look at past paper questions, and exam board specimen questions, to familiarize yourself with the type of question that is specific to the exam you are going to take.

You will have to practise reading the printed extract really carefully and squeezing every last drop of meaning out of it.

When you are practising writing answers to extract-based questions, use a pen or highlighter to underline key words and phrases from the extract that will be important in your response. It can also be helpful to write very brief notes in the margins of the extract, so you remember what the highlights refer to.

Spend up to five minutes on this.

Here is an example of how a candidate might have highlighted an extract.

---

powerful verbs
and emotive
adjectives describe
horror of war

I explode into wakefulness along with the booming artillery and I find myself gasping, instantly wide-eyed, not cold for once, in Mrs Belander's tenement, the sweat warm on my flesh, but in a minute the sweat turns icy. In the alley that day, I encountered the German soldiers, all right, but my bursts of gunfire killed the soldiers quickly, no exploding head, no body cut in two, although one of them cried Mama as he fell. When I looked down at them, in one of those eerie pauses that happens in an attack — a sudden silence that's even more terrible than exploding

youth of soldiers
emphasized

shells — I saw how young they were, boys with apple cheeks, too young to shave. Like me.

You can also use either of these methods in the exam itself, but remember never to use highlighters in your own answers.

Step 4: Answering the question

Always make a careful plan before you start writing an essay-based answer. If you are answering an extract-based question, read the passage very carefully, annotating the extract as suggested above before you begin your answer. An essay plan will help you to:

- structure your answer logically
- target the precise demands of the question
- avoid missing out points that are crucial to your argument
- include appropriate quotations.

Plans can take a variety of forms (lists, spider diagrams, etc.). However, a brief list is often the most helpful as it allows you to put ideas in a logical sequence and you can deal with each idea at a time.

Don't spend more than about 6 or 7 minutes on a plan. The first few minutes are 'thinking time' – then jot down your ideas and away you go!

Always write a brief introduction that is directly focused on the question. So, if the question asks: 'Do you consider Larry LaSalle to be a hero, a villain or both in *Heroes*?' you might write:

I consider Larry LaSalle to be a hero in some parts of the novel and a villain in other parts of 'Heroes'.

Develop your answer, step by step, building your argument by referring to precise moments from the novel. With *Heroes*, you can refer to events by 'time frame', for example:

> Larry is presented in a flashback as Francis recalls his arrival as leader of the Wreck Centre.

Always support your ideas with short, relevant quotations from the novel. The best way to use a quotation is to 'absorb' it into your own sentences. For example:

> When Larry leaves the Wreck Centre after raping Nicole, he is 'whistling softly'; this suggests a carefree attitude and so helps to emphasize the callousness of the planned assault. This is one aspect of Larry's villainy.

Notice how, in this example, the student locates a clear moment of action that suggests that Larry is a 'villain'; the student quotes briefly but purposefully from the novel and explains how the quotation contributes to the impression that Larry is a villain at this point. Close focus on the question is achieved.

It is possible to 'absorb' longer quotations into your sentences as well. For example:

> At the end of Chapter 14, Cormier asks us to reflect whether Larry is a hero or a villain when Francis hears Larry's 'voice' echoing in his ears and asking, "Does that one sin of mine wipe away all the good things?"

Keep track of time in the exam. Make sure you know in advance how much time you can spend on each part of the paper and stick to it! Remember to factor in time for planning. Do all you can to avoid leaving an answer unfinished. Examiners rarely credit notes or bullet points. It is always better to end your answer with a short, neat conclusion that reminds the examiner that you have done what you were asked to do. For example:

> Although Larry LaSalle does a horrible thing to Nicole when he rapes her, I do not believe that he is a complete villain. I have shown how his better qualities of encouraging the young people at the Wreck Centre, of fighting for his country and of boosting Francis's low self-esteem make him rather a 'fallen' hero.

Sample questions

1

Foundation Tier

Heroes

Either a)

Explain the importance of Larry LaSalle in the novel. In your answer, you **must** consider:

- his relationships with young people in the Wreck Centre
- his actions during the war
- how he is perceived by Francis and how he is perceived by others.

You may include other ideas of your own.

Use **evidence** to support your answer.

Or b)

How are guilt and forgiveness presented in the novel? In your answer, you **must** consider:

- references in the novel to sin and redemption
- Francis's guilt over Nicole's attack
- guilt and forgiveness experienced by other characters in the novel.

You may include other ideas of your own.

Use **evidence** to support your answer.

2

Higher Tier

Heroes

Either a)

In what ways is the character of Larry LaSalle significant in the novel?

You **must** consider the context of the novel.

Use **evidence** to support your answer.

Or b)

Explore the significance of guilt and forgiveness in the novel.

You **must** consider the context of the novel.

Use **evidence** to support your answer.

3

Foundation Tier

Heroes

Answer question (a) and **either** part (b) **or** part (c).

a) *Look at the extract in Chapter 11 from 'She saw me the moment I saw her' to the end of the chapter.*

What are your thoughts and feelings as you read this extract?

Either

b) What do you think about Nicole Renard?
Think about:

- her relationship with Francis
- how she is described in the novel
- what happens to her at the Wreck Centre
- the way she speaks and behaves at different points in the novel.

Or

c) What impressions do you get of Frenchtown?
Think about:

- the people who live there
- what happens there
- how the town is described
- anything else you think important.

4

Higher Tier

Heroes

Answer question (a) and **either** part (b) **or** part (c).

a) *Look at the extract in Chapter 11 from 'She saw me the moment I saw her' to the end of the chapter.*

With close reference to the extract, show how Robert Cormier creates mood and atmosphere here.

Either

b) What do you think of Nicole Renard and the way she is presented in the novel?

Or

c) How does Robert Cormier present the town of Frenchtown in *Heroes*?

Sample answers

Sample answer 1

Below you will find a sample response from a **Foundation Tier** student, together with examiner comments, to the following general question on the novel:

> Why do you think Robert Cormier chose to call his novel 'Heroes'?

I think Cormier calls his novel 'Heroes' because Francis is always talking about heroes and telling us that he isn't one.

Shows some awareness of the prominence of the theme of heroes.

I actually think that Francis was a hero because he saved the lives of his platoon and, even if he had died, the army would probably have given him a medal that would have been sent to his Uncle Louis in Canada, so he would still have been a hero. If this had happened, Nicole may of wished that he had come back to marry her because she wouldn't have seen his face all burned up. Then she would of felt guilty about blaming Francis for not saving her at the Wreck Centre.

While this is outside the scope of the novel, it does reveal some awareness of the official 'recognition' of heroism.

This is speculation and not creditworthy.

Grammar could have been improved.

Francis didn't save Nicole from Larry because he was only a child and could not of beaten Larry if he had tried to stop him. We had been told that Larry came back on leave very thin and 'lethal', which meant that Francis could not of beaten him. He was also a 'silver star' hero so there was no stopping him.

Brief quotation and an attempt to link the idea of being a hero with Francis's sense of helplessness.

I also think he called it 'Heroes' because the novel includes other kinds of heroes like baseball players and even Francis is a table tennis champion at the Wreck Centre.

Shows some focus on the question here.

Larry is the hero of all the kids at the Wreck Centre where he brings out the best in people until he turns bad and rapes Nicole.

Gives a somewhat simplistic point here, which needs development.

When Francis comes to shoot him, I think that Larry is still a hero because he kills himself to stop Francis being a murderer.

Makes a better point but one that needs support from the text.

This is a mixed response with occasional focus on the demands of the question. Expression is not always secure.

Sample answer 2

Below you will find a sample response from a **Higher Tier** student, together with examiner comments, to the same general question on the novel.

> Why do you think Robert Cormier chose to call his novel 'Heroes'?

Shows clear focus on the question.

Cormier's title of 'Heroes' is very effective because it makes the reader think, from the very beginning, about what heroism is.

This is a good paragraph with a range of useful examples.

In the course of the novel, the reader meets a number of characters who might be considered brave, for example, Enrico Rucelli, who tries to keep cheerful in spite of his terrible injuries and Nicole, who doesn't speak about the rape but who makes a fresh start in Albany and remains committed to becoming a teacher. Cormier also refers frequently to characters who have been high achievers in sport or film and he suggests that they are a type of 'hero' to their followers and fans. The Strangler keeps a scrapbook of 'Frenchtown warriors' and seems to think that every Frenchtown man or woman who joined the forces is automatically a hero.

However, Larry LaSalle and Francis are the only two characters we meet who actually have medals for heroism and each has been awarded the special 'Silver Star' for having saved the lives of several men in their platoons.

Good focus.

Shows clear work on the contrasting 'heroes'.

Cormier uses these very different characters to demonstrate contrasting examples of heroes. Larry is definitely presented as a character more likely to become a hero than Francis. He arrives in Frenchtown, as described in Chapter 5, ready to take over the Wreck Centre as its leader. Cormier gives Larry dashing looks, including, 'dazzling movie-star teeth', 'the broad shoulders of an athlete and the narrow hips of a dancer'. He has been a star in the nightclubs of New York and Chicago and his presence in Frenchtown is inspirational to the young people, including Francis. By contrast, Francis is one of 'the shorter kids', 'without talent for singing or dancing or arts and crafts', he is awkward and tongue-tied around Nicole; he is a lonely orphan whose main occupation is reading.

Cormier contrasts Larry and Francis to highlight the theme of heroes. When Larry enlists in Chapter 9, he makes a public announcement of his decision and although the kids want to cheer him, he modestly refuses their admiration, stating 'I'm just doing what millions of others are doing'. When he returns on furlough, it is to a hero's reception, hosted by the Mayor of Monument.

Shows consistent attention to Cormier's intentions.

In contrast, Francis enlists with the clear intention to kill himself, to escape from his shame over betraying Nicole and his sense of being a coward. He forges his birth certificate and slips away. His return to Frenchtown is equally low key. Unannounced, despite his 'silver star', Francis wants to be anonymous and is pleased when he is not recognized, not even by his old neighbour Mrs Belander, who baked him a cake for his thirteenth birthday.

Even when Francis is recognized by Arthur, he refuses to allow him to disclose his identity and it is clear that Francis does not consider himself to be a hero – a comment that he makes repeatedly throughout the novel.

Secure knowledge of the novel is evident.

One of the most important chapters about heroism, and the one that most suggests how right and effective 'Heroes' is as the title of the novel, is Chapter 14 where Francis confronts Larry about his past and Larry kills himself. Francis tells Larry, 'I'm not a hero', and tells the reader he had been 'a fake all along'. In return, Larry is shocked to discover how much his actions disgust Francis and he admits how much he enjoyed being idolized by the kids at the Wreck Centre, saying 'If I want one thing, it would be to have you look at me again the way you did at the Wreck Centre. When I was the big hero you say I was.'

Very good choice of examples.

It seems important that here Larry is not claiming to be a hero, but he appreciates that he was a hero in Francis's eyes. This moment is central to the whole novel which seems to conclude that heroism is very much in the 'eye of the beholder' and that, whether or not he believes it, we see Francis, with his horribly disfigured face and strong sense of right and wrong to be the hero of this novel.

This is very perceptive and well expressed.

This is a very assured piece of work, which is both perceptive and well expressed.

Sample answer 3

Read the extract below taken from a student response, together with examiner comments, to the following sample **Foundation Tier** question:

> How are guilt and forgiveness presented in the novel? In your answer, you **must** consider:
>
> - references in the novel to sin and redemption
> - Francis's guilt over Nicole's attack
> - guilt and forgiveness experienced by other characters in the novel.
>
> You may include other ideas of your own.
> Use **evidence** to support your answer.

A good introduction, which shows understanding of the task.

Robert Cormier presents guilt and forgiveness in a few different ways in his novel 'Heroes'. Francis, the narrator, feels a lot of guilt over what happens to Nicole, but strangely Larry LaSalle, who assaults her, does not seem to feel guilty even though his actions cause Francis to join the army and lose his face.

Useful focus on the writer's methods.

One thing Cormier does is to compare these two characters. Larry LaSalle is obviously guilty of betraying the children at the Wreck Centre who he was supposed to be protecting. Francis, on the other hand, is obviously innocent, even though he is the one who feels the most guilt.

This paragraph addresses the need to refer to context efficiently.

In the book, there are many references to sin and redemption. This is because of the context of the book – the Catholic community of Frenchtown. The values of the Church, with its clear ideas about sin, guilt and forgiveness, form the rules that people live by. Francis believes that he is guilty for not stopping Larry from raping Nicole.

An interesting suggestion, which is supported from the text.

The bag could also be seen as a symbol of Francis's guilt, since at the end of the novel, when he knows he has been forgiven by Nicole, and after Larry has killed himself, he finds the duffel bag 'nice and comfortable on my back' which might show that his 'guilt' has lifted.

This shows understanding.

Useful reference to text here.

Francis may feel guilty about his 'sin of omission' in not going to Nicole's rescue but he is shocked to discover, when he confronts Larry about his crime in Chapter 14 that Larry feels no guilt at all for what he has done to Nicole. Larry didn't feel guilty at the time since even after raping an innocent girl, he left the building 'whistling softly' the tune of 'Dancing in the Dark'.

This is a good response to the question. It is not wide-ranging but it is focused precisely on the question and a number of different methods are considered. It would benefit from better organization.

Sample answer 4

Read the extract below taken from a student response, together with examiner comments, to the following sample **Higher Tier** question:

> **a)** *Look at the extract in Chapter 11 from 'She saw me the moment I saw her' to the end of the chapter.*
>
> With close reference to the extract, show how Robert Cormier creates mood and atmosphere here.

The extract is very important in the novel as Francis realizes that he has betrayed Nicole by doing nothing. He has heard noises that sound like Nicole is being raped by Larry but he is paralysed by panic.

A useful context is offered here.

In this novel, Cormier often refers to faces. Francis tells us that he has 'no face' in Chapter 1 but he notices other faces throughout. The way in which Cormier lists separate parts of Nicole ('hair dishevelled, mouth flung open, lips swollen. Cheeks moist') draws attention to Nicole's face and how it has been hurt by Larry. There is tension as we do not know what else Cormier will tell us about the assault. Nicole's white blouse, which was a symbol of her purity, is now 'torn' and the word 'clutching' makes Nicole sound scared as she tries to protect herself. This fear adds to the tension.

Gives useful reference to the wider novel.

Keeps focus on the question.

Keeps focus on the question.

Cormier creates tension by stressing the darkness that surrounds Nicole and Francis, and we don't know what Larry might do when he discovers Francis in the foyer. When Francis moves towards her, Nicole's 'gasping' also creates tension as it reveals her fear even at seeing Francis, while the 'moan' recalls the noises that we were told about in Chapter 5 when the history of the 'Wreck Centre' was first narrated and the tradition of children listening at the door for 'moaning and weeping' was described as a 'rite of passage'. By using the same word here, Cormier reminds the reader of the violent history of the place and tension increases as we wonder what else might happen here.

Maintains consistent focus on the question.

Shows excellent awareness of the place of the extract in the novel as a whole.

Another way that Cormier creates tension here is through the narrative technique because he is writing as if he is Francis and doesn't actually know whether Larry has seen him or not. He seems to speak directly to the reader ('Had he seen me?'), but if he doesn't know, how can we?

Shows personal engagement and insight.

A very sound response to the extract; perceptive comments with good textual support.

Glossary

alliteration the repetition of the same letter or sound at the beginning of words close to one another

allusion (in literature) a reference to other literary texts such as plays, poems or novels or to specific literary traditions

antagonist a character or group of characters whose function in a story is to oppose the main character (protagonist)

anti-hero a main character who has significant bad qualities, but whom the reader finds it difficult to condemn because of their good or attractive ones

antithesis contrasting ideas or words that are balanced against one another

aside a speech in a play given by an actor directly to the audience, unheard by the other characters (in this context, Francis's unspoken thoughts)

atmosphere the mood created by a piece of writing

atonement something that is done to make amends for a wrong action; it is supposed to help to 'wipe away' a sin

Bildungsroman a literary genre focused around the main character's psychological and moral growth

chronological narrative the presentation of events in a story in the order in which they actually occurred

climax a turning point in the action of a novel; the moment where the action or crisis reaches its greatest intensity

colloquial language informal, everyday speech

coming of age growing into adulthood through knowledge and experience

connotation an association created by a word – not its actual meaning, but ideas or qualities it implies

figurative language the collective name for simile, metaphor and personification; language which is not to be taken literally

first-person narration a story told from the narrator's point of view, using the pronouns 'I' or 'me'

flashback a sudden recollection of a previous event that shifts the action back into the past

foil a character whose function in a story is to serve as a contrast to another character, in order to highlight one of their qualities

furlough approved time off from military service

irony the discrepancy between what a character could be expected to do and what they actually do, often for comic effect

memory the recollection of a past event in the present; the action is not transported back to the past, although memories give the reader an insight into Francis' past experiences

metaphor a comparison of one thing to another to make a description more vivid; a metaphor states that one thing is the other

mortal sin in the Catholic church, a sin that condemns the sinner to Hell

motif a repeated idea, phrase or word that the reader notices again and again in a text, and which supports the themes in a text

narrative structure the way in which a writer organizes a story to create meaning

narrative technique a method that a novelist uses to tell his or her story

narrator the person who tells a story (Francis is the narrator in *Heroes*)

omniscient narrator a narrator who knows everything about the characters that he or she is writing about, including their inner thoughts and motivations, usually written in the third person

onomatopoeia the use of words which sound like the thing or process they describe

personification a type of metaphor where human qualities are given to objects or ideas

simile a comparison of one thing to another to make a description more vivid, using the words 'like' or 'as' to make the comparison

sin of omission in Catholic terminology, knowing the right thing to do, being capable of doing it and yet failing to do it

synaesthesia a literary device where words associated with one sense are used to describe another sense

veteran an experienced serviceman or woman who has served in the military forces; note that, while the term can also imply age (e.g. veteran cars), ironically the majority of veterans in *Heroes* are in their late teens or early twenties

Great Clarendon Street, Oxford OX2 6DP

Oxford University Press is a department of the University of Oxford.
It furthers the University's objective of excellence in research,
scholarship, and education by publishing worldwide in

Oxford   New York

Auckland   Cape Town   Dar es Salaam   Hong Kong   Karachi
Kuala Lumpur   Madrid   Melbourne   Mexico City   Nairobi
New Delhi   Shanghai   Taipei   Toronto

With offices in

Argentina   Austria   Brazil   Chile   Czech Republic   France   Greece
Guatemala   Hungary   Italy   Japan   Poland   Portugal   Singapore
South Korea   Switzerland   Thailand   Turkey   Ukraine   Vietnam

Oxford is a registered trade mark of Oxford University Press
in the UK and in certain other countries

© Su Fielder 2012

The moral rights of the author have been asserted

Database right Oxford University Press (maker)

First published 2012

British Library Cataloguing in Publication Data

Data available

ISBN 978-0-19-912877-8

10 9 8 7 6 5 4 3 2

Printed by Vivar Printing Sdn Bhd., Malaysia

Acknowledgements
The publisher and author are grateful for permission to reprint the
following copyright material:

Extracts from Robert Cormier: *Heroes* (Hamish Hamilton 1998), copyright
© Robert Cormier 1998, reprinted by permission of Penguin Books Ltd.

Cover: ©Bettmann/Corbis; **p7:** The Art Archive/Alamy; **p10:** Trinity
Mirror/Mirrorpix/Alamy; **p13:** Natale/Shutterstock; **p17:** US Army. Mil;
p21: Trinity Mirror/Mirrorpix/Alamy; **p25:** The Art Gallery Collection/
Alamy; **p28:** Peter Stackpole/Time & Life Pictures/Getty Images; **p32:**
itanistock/Alamy; **p36:** De Agostini/Getty Images; **p39:** ©Bettmann/
Corbis; **p42:** Travel Pictures/Alamy; **p49:** Joe Vogan/Alamy; **p52:**
PhotoAlto/Alamy; **p57:** Graham Morley/Alamy; **p60:** AF archive/Alamy;
p63: Mary Evans Picture Library/Alamy.